THIRTEEN LESSONS THAT SAVED
THIRTEEN LIVES

THIRTEEN LESSONS THAT SAVED
THIRTEEN LIVES
THE THAI CAVE RESCUE

JOHN VOLANTHEN
With Matt Allen

Aurum

First published in paperback in 2022 by Aurum
an imprint of The Quarto Group.

The Old Brewery, 6 Blundell Street,
London, N7 9BH, United Kingdom.
www.QuartoKnows.com/Aurum

A catalogue record for this book is available from the British Library.

ISBN: 978-07112-6610-0
E-book ISBN: 978-0-7112-6611-7

1 2 3 4 5 6 7 8 9 10

Cover design by Luke Bird
Typeset in Adobe Caslon Pro by SX Composing DTP, Rayleigh, Essex, SS6 7EF
Printed and bound by CPI Group (UK) Ltd, Croydon, CR0 4YY

CONTENTS

INTRODUCTION

They were alive.

I counted all thirteen faces with my flashlight as they peered back through the gloom. *One: Titan. Two: Mix. Three: Dom. Four: Pong.* Stuck inside a cave for nearly two weeks, unsurprisingly they looked tired and frightened. *Five: Mark. Six: Tern. Seven: Biw. Eight: Adul. Nine: Note. Ten: Nick.* T-shirts hung from their malnourished bodies as they shuffled towards us like ghouls: waving, pointing, almost disbelieving that anyone could have emerged from the chilly underground floodwaters that had trapped them for the best part of a fortnight. *Eleven: Tee. Twelve: Night. And finally, number thirteen, the Wild Boars football team coach, Ek.* This was a group of boys the world had already written off as dead. The football team stuck on a small bank in the belly of Tham Luang, a sidewinding labyrinth of caves positioned underneath the Doi Nang Non mountain range on the border between Thailand and Myanmar, and impenetrable to any rescue attempts – *until now.*

Some of the kids shouted out.

'Thank you,' yelled a voice at the back.

'Are we going out today?' said another, waving into the inky darkness.

The smallest boy in the group slumped to the ground and sobbed silently. The poor kid looked distraught, which came as no great surprise given it was 2 July 2018 and the kids, aged between eleven and seventeen, plus twenty-five-year-old Ek, had first been reported missing on 23 June 2018. According to news reports, the date had been important. Night was celebrating his seventeenth birthday and the plan had been for an hour-long group excursion into the cave. For the Wild Boars, this was a big deal. Night had been the first of the team to reach such a milestone age; he was the oldest member in the group and the other boys looked up to him. Meanwhile, Ek, the responsible adult, had come along to guide everybody through the tunnels. The feeling was that all the boys within the group would be in safe hands.

The chances are, had anyone known that the previous day's heavy storms were still filling the caves with floodwater, they would have warned the Wild Boars off such an excursion. Under those circumstances, crawling inside was incredibly risky because cave systems like Tham Luang held an unnerving reputation. On a bad day they could flood quickly, and with lethal results. What might have seemed like a fairly innocuous team adventure into the dark on a grey, but hot afternoon, a cool way to hang out after football training, very quickly twisted into a nightmarish ordeal as waves of churning water surged through the narrow tunnels at high speed, transforming a series of interlinking caverns into watery tombs. Escaping on foot was suddenly unimaginable.

Claustrophobic, narrow cracks in the rock, and passages that had seemed like a tight squeeze on the way in had become sunken death traps. Every escape route was impossible to negotiate without underwater breathing apparatus, serious experience and a steady nerve, so there was certainly no way out for a bunch of kids with zero knowledge of cave diving. Climbing to higher ground inside the cavern in search of safety, the waters around them still rising, the Wild Boars had huddled together for warmth instead. Prayer was all they had left. The team would need rescuing, that's if anybody knew they'd entered the cave at all.

But they did. After twenty-four hours, the story of their disappearance started to creep across news feeds all over the world. Very soon, TV crews and journalists were flying to Thailand. Online, people were issuing their hopes, prayers and platitudes. And it was because of the news that I had decided to offer my services, having eventually figured out that given our experience and expertise in such high-pressure situations, my regular diving partner Rick Stanton and I were best placed to conduct a search and rescue mission. All my cave rescues had been unpaid. Rather than a career, I had always considered these operations as my contribution to what was a small community of divers. For work I ran my own IT business. In Thailand I was a volunteer.

But commitments of this kind had certainly led me on an interesting journey. I'd been a cave diver for thirty-odd years, and alongside Rick I had set two records[*]. The first was for diving 76 metres (249 feet) into Wookey Hole, Somerset in 2004 – the greatest depth recorded in a British cave. I then broke the record for the longest exploration into a cave when, as a team we dived 8,800 metres (28,900 feet) into the Pozo Azul caverns in Spain's Rudrón Valley in 2010. Rick and I worked together regularly. We first dived as part of a team in Gough's Cave, Somerset, during 2002, where I'd carried in a series of diving cylinders for weeks to help explore the end of the cave. In a single

---

[*] UK cave divers will usually explore alone. Sometimes they deliberately put distance between themselves and any other divers underwater. This might seem counter-intuitive, but in small passages with low visibility, a buddy or partner can often be a hindrance to solving problems.

dive, Rick was able not only to visit, but to extend the end of the tunnels and I realised that he'd built his own rebreather* to do so. I decided that constructing one of my own was a vital next step; the alternative was to hang up my fins. I chose the former, and a strong partnership developed between the two of us.

Together, Rick and I had previously conducted a number of high-profile rescue operations, as well as volunteering to work in body recovery missions, a grizzly business, and as a result I had developed the skill set, confidence and knowhow to execute the job. But having arrived in Thailand and negotiated the political machinations surrounding what should have been a fairly straightforward humanitarian effort, and having spent several days attempting to find the stricken team, I had come to fear the worst. During dives I had to wriggle against murky, churning currents and through body-hugging cracks in the rock, my head torch unable to pierce the murky water. Tham Luang felt impenetrable.

'There's no chance those kids have survived,' I thought after one particularly gruelling dive. '*Is there?*'

One night I even went so far as to mentally prepare myself for a hellish, endgame event. I visualised swimming into a tunnel choked with what looked like discarded plastic bags, ragged clothing and shoes, only to realise it was an underwater morgue. Mentally, the process, though morbid, steeled me for the grimmest of outcomes, but I wasn't the only one preparing for such a negative event. The Thai authorities had all but given up hope, too, and the mood within the divers I'd been working alongside was just as doom-laden – a group that included my diving partner

---

* A device that recycles the diver's exhaled breath, removing carbon dioxide and adding oxygen. It is very much more efficient than open-circuit regulators at depth.

Rick, Belgian cave diver Ben Reymenants, plus units from the Thai Navy SEALs, some members of the US military and a handful of Australian police divers. It was a widely shared view among us all that once the waters had retreated from Tham Luang, some of the group would be faced with the unenviable task of fishing a number of corpses from the muddy pools.

But we'd been wrong. *Those kids had made it.*

In the end, when Rick and I had located the Wild Boars' whereabouts, it had an unlikely feel to it. On 30 June, word filtered through to the rescue teams that our efforts had gone as far as they could, and so a colleague took us on a day trip around the mountain, even as the storm was still raging around us. I was quite happy for the distraction: we had been trapped by circumstance and bureaucracy, and the Thai government, keen not to create a PR disaster, wanted to hold all the foreign volunteer teams on site. Their fear was that a photo of the rescuers might be taken as they packed away equipment and tidied up their kit. That image would send an international message that thirteen lives had been lost and the authorities had been powerless to help.

Then everything changed. The weather calmed a little and the rapids that had once held us back from pushing deeper in to the Tham Luang tunnels began a slow retreat. We decided to make one more attempt at finding the Wild Boars. Supported by the American and Thai rescue teams in attendance, we spent two days swimming further into the caverns and fixing guidelines – the kind of rope you might see used on a mountain expedition as a team of high-altitude climbers attack the summit of some inaccessible peak. Underwater in a cave, however, these ropes worked in two ways. The first was to serve as a route marker in the churning, sediment-heavy waters. The second was as a tool for forward momentum: by pulling on the line, a following diver could move more easily past stalactites and stalagmites, through rocky, body-hugging tubes and into vast pools with no immediate escape routes. If you haven't guessed already, cave rescues are no task for the faint-hearted.

As the search progressed and the floodwaters retreated, little by little, Rick and I realised that we were suddenly able to penetrate much further into the cave than any previous dive had managed so far. The bad news was that time was against us. We had been working through the cave for five hours. Our air supply was fading, and I knew we needed to turn around if we were to make it back to the cave entrance safely. As the famous mountain climber, Ed Viesturs had once claimed, 'Getting to the top of Everest is optional. Getting down is mandatory.' A similar theory applies to cave diving.

Let me explain. Once a diver had hit a certain level in his air tanks, even with rebreathing equipment – the air mask and tank that recycled used air to create a near constant supply – they then had to commit to making the journey home. (The golden rule is to think in thirds: one-third of a tank for the way in; one-third for the way out; one-third for emergencies.) Having pushed past what were my normal and acceptable safety margins, while laying out nearly all the guideline as we moved deeper into Tham Luang, I'd reached my turning point. The water was getting cold and the grim visualisation exercise I'd undertaken a few days earlier seemed set to transform into a horrific reality. While moving through a dark sump*, my vision distorted by rushing

---

* A flooded section of cave passage where the water reaches the roof.

water and churning mud, I bumped into a heavy object moving in the current. Then something brushed against my legs.

'Oh, God,' I thought. 'Have I just found the first body?'

I kicked forward into the murk and spotted what I thought was a skeletal limb floating towards me. It bobbed and swayed in the currents. *Was I going to find a torso, a head, and a pair of legs as well?* My stomach tensed. I reached forward to make a grab for it, my breath slowing as the lifeless shape in the gloom turned out to be nothing more than a discarded length of rubber piping. Not that I felt any less concerned. As ominous signs nudged me in the currents, an unpleasant discovery seemed inevitable.

With each passing minute, my desire to turn back only mounted further. I even prayed that the rope I had been feeding into the caves might run out – because we would have to return to the safety of the entrance once the last of our guidelines had been set. But then the passage roof seemed to rise up. We had emerged into another large air pocket and I immediately took in our surroundings. We were in a dark cavern and the scene around me seemed so different to the murky underworld we'd been moving through a second or two earlier.

The cave was large and only half-filled with water. There was no light, apart from the beam of my head torch, but I felt a sensory jolt; a weird signal that everything around us was *different*. More than anything, there was an immediate, instinctive feeling that an unusual happening was in motion. At first it was intangible. There was a flicker in my peripheral vision. I sensed movement nearby. *Was someone watching us?* Then I noticed Rick. He'd taken off his face mask. As his head turned this way and that, I noticed his nostrils flaring. *He was sniffing the air.*

'Take a smell,' he said, pointing to the cavern's dark corners. 'Tell me what you get . . .'

The stink, when I inhaled deeply, was heavy, ripe and strong enough to twist the stomach. 'Oh no, Rick. That's rotting flesh.'

He nodded sombrely. We had finally discovered what we'd assumed would be a graveyard.

Except, we hadn't.

There was a sound behind me, then another. As I twisted around it was hard to take in the reality of what was happening. A group of boys had gathered silently at the water's edge and were pointing. *It was the Wild Boars!* It had to be . . . *But, how?* With barely any food between them, or a proper source of drinking water, it seemed unthinkable that they could have survived for ten days. Certainly, very few people in the rescue team had fancied their chances – and yet, here they were. I couldn't believe they had made it through the flood.

Instinctively, I shouted across to them. 'How many of you?'

There was no response, but I could hear Rick counting. 'One, two, three . . .'

Moving closer to the bank, I shone my head torch towards the faces looking back at me.

'Eleven, twelve, thirteen . . . *They're all here.*'

Brilliant.

But the situation had unsettled me a little and, at first, I felt overwhelmed by the enormity of what to do next. I had no idea of how we were going to transport the team back to safety in what would be a gruelling swim of around four hours, with the current behind us. Then, I mentally broke the situation down into manageable phases. Assessing the health and wellbeing of the stranded team had to be the first priority. Apart from Ek, the coach, the Wild Boars were kids; they were starved, which meant they would be close to their physical and emotional breaking points, though given the different ages within the group, some would undoubtedly be tougher than others. I knew that Rick had a Snickers bar shoved into his wetsuit pocket, but dishing it out at that point would have only created a *Lord of the Flies*-style conflict, in which the strongest boys feasted on small bites of chocolate while the weakest starved.

Reading the room, and guessing the implications of handing out the measliest of food parcels, Rick pushed the chocolate bar further into his suit. From now on, paying close attention to the tiniest details would be key, but building morale was just as important. As a volunteer with the Somerset Cub Scouts, I had gathered a fair level of experience in working alongside kids in challenging, outdoor environments: I often took groups caving where there was the possibility that somebody might lose their nerve, or experience a minor meltdown while exploring what could be a fairly intimidating environment. To succeed in Tham Luang I would need to apply similar levels of empathy, plus a good bedside manner as the situation unfolded around me. *I would pretend the Wild Boars were Cub Scouts.* In which case, it was important to reassure them by presenting confidence and authority.

'We are coming,' I said, hoping to pass on the idea that their survival wasn't entirely dependent on the actions of two middle-aged blokes from England. 'Many people are coming. Believe . . .'

I said it again, to make absolutely sure they understood. '*Believe.*'

Every action and gesture was being captured on a headcam given to us by the Thai Navy SEALs, and during the rescue's aftermath, a lot of people watching the footage emailed me to express their gratitude. They believed my sole intention at that moment had been to reassure the boys that they were found and that people would soon be working to extract them. Full disclosure: while that was undoubtedly true, there was another, more selfish motive for pushing the idea. *I was trying to convince myself.*

I needed to underline the new reality. Not five minutes earlier, I had been hoping to turn around for home. I was tired, overwhelmed and drained after a tumultuous week, having dived, pulled and crawled through a flooded subterranean maze for hours on end. Now I was presented with the daunting prospect of evacuating a football team of boys through an environment that had already defeated some of the most experienced special forces operators in Thailand, not to mention a number of resilient military divers from around the world.

Considered as a whole, the job certainly should have been beyond Rick and myself. As far as we knew, the stranded kids were unable to swim, let alone navigate their way through the challenging and potentially lethal, watery arteries of Tham Luang with its limited visibility and surging currents. They were also malnourished and frail. That meant there was a high chance, given their weakened state, that the water would turn them hypothermic very quickly. The nightmarish scenario that at least one of them would panic underwater was also a major worry. For now, though, I had to compartmentalise my emotions and prepare for a phase of planning. Leaving the Wild Boars with our spare flashlights, Rick and I hugged the children in turn, then headed back into the flood to tell the waiting rescue teams what we had found. But the pair of us had become linked to those starving, frightened kids with one shared thought.

Believe.

It was now my job to turn that belief into something approaching reality.

Thirteen lives depended on it. Luckily, I had thirteen hard-learned lessons to lean upon.

They would eventually prove the difference between success and tragedy.

■ ■ ■

Here is an inescapable reality: at one time or another, all of us will face what might feel like an insurmountable challenge. In my case, I had to help extract those thirteen stricken people from a drowned cave; another individual's test might present itself as something less dramatic, but equally daunting. Maybe they're fighting a life-threatening condition, or returning from a serious physical or emotional injury. It might be that someone has been tasked with organising a project or event of massive importance; or they have decided to take on a potentially overwhelming life change, such as a move abroad or a shift away from their long-term career.

Each person in a moment of this kind will come face-to-face with the risk/reward conundrum: as with my rescue efforts in Thailand, challenges always arrive loaded with consequences, and that can be a cause for worry. The upside is that the rewards for executing such a task can be satisfying, empowering or even life-changing. Luckily, as I've learned through a life spent rescuing stricken individuals and exploring some of the most impenetrable places on the planet, the psychological skills required to succeed are fairly universal and incredibly translatable to the challenges we all face in our lives.

At this point, you might be wondering, 'How can a bloody cave diver help me with some of *my* struggles?' Fair point. But the answer can be found in the very nature of what I do. Typically, cave divers are problem-solvers, fixers, and thinkers. The very idea of swimming into a series of flooded tunnels, entirely unsure of where they might lead or whether they will finish in a tricky dead end with next to no room to turn around, is what excites some people. (Not all, but some. And from what I've learned about myself over the years, I can definitely be bracketed in the 'some' category.) As far as I'm concerned, the appeal is entirely understandable. Cave diving requires an individual to think under pressure to see an idea or plan through to the end. I have spent my time underwater pushing that idea to the limit.

Being part of a cave-rescue team or an exploration group has required me to learn many hard lessons while developing a number of key skills. I have discovered that among the traits required to operate in such a challenging environment is a healthy sense of focus, as well an awareness of the dangers regarding *overfocus*. I've learned to cope with task loading – a situation in which an individual faces a large number of seemingly simple processes at once. If he or she is not careful, the capacity to manage those processes can quickly diminish. Understanding when a challenge is exposing me to unacceptable risk and then immediately changing course has also become important.

The most successful cave divers appreciate the importance of taking responsibility at all times (while handling the fears created by committing to that responsibility). They also know how to break a big problem down into a series of smaller, more manageable events, and I have often leant into the concepts of teamwork and trust, visualisation and rehearsal and the all-important benefits of rest and decompression. These ideas are really tools that every cave diver has to employ if they are to explore and map previously untouched caves, or even rescue a trapped diver. But those same tools can be transferred to any challenge, or a crisis situation away from a cave, where life can be just as turbulent and unpredictable. In the coming chapters I will explain how.

On the surface, *Thirteen Lessons That Saved Thirteen Lives* details exactly how we were able to save the Wild Boars in what was the most challenging rescue mission of my life. But it also reveals a simple-to-follow set of processes that can be used when facing up to any test, big or small. This starts with acceptance. We're all guilty of listening to the subconscious and self-defeating whispers of the Inner Critic; that snide, nagging presence that says: *'But you can't . . .'* And it's a hard voice to ignore, especially when the negative chatter begins during a nerve-wracking moment, such that first-time house buy, or before a presentation of innovative, but unpopular business ideas. However, to succeed, we must acknowledge the test and its difficulties, and then respond with an affirmative action. Or, in other words, react to the Inner Critic with force and one simple statement: *'Yes, I can!'* And while this is only a first step, and there's plenty of work to complete afterwards, beyond that simple gesture lies a usually transformative moment.

I have come to understand this process well because cave diving has thrust me into some very daunting situations and the most dramatic and testing of events. During potentially life-threatening experiences at depth, I learned about time slicing and how to think by taking one breath at a time. I discovered the pressure of taking responsibility for someone else's life for the first time when supporting my dive partner, Rick, during what would become a nerve-wracking exploration of Saint-Sauveur in France in 2007. The dangers of becoming overfocused became worryingly apparent during my record-breaking exploration dive of Wookey Hole in 2004: having spent my resources working to move a boulder so I could swim even deeper into the cave, I became disorientated and blinded in the dark brown waters. Elsewhere, I experienced moments of self-discovery regarding uncertainty, pressure and stress; I learned about the importance of self-awareness, commitment, and finding value in defeat. Overall, though, there has been discovery in transforming the seemingly impossible into something more achievable. Applying these lessons, and others detailed in this book, helped me to rescue the Wild Boars in Tham Luang.

This achievement in itself proves the power of an education received underwater, because I have never considered myself to be extraordinary in any way. You might have guessed from my photo that I am not the physically overwhelming, war-hero type. I am not one for telling people how to 'crush it' in boardroom meetings, either. Instead, I am a very real example of what happens when sheer willpower meets the statement, 'But I can't . . .' head on, because I have worked through that tipping point many times myself. I was bullied as a kid and later downtrodden by people who considered me an outsider, or as odd. Because I lacked confidence, for a while I found it hard to accept the thought that I could rise up to any challenge.

Like most people, when life events spiralled out of control, I worked hard to correct those situations as best I could, and with varying degrees of success. But when things did actually go my way, I assumed that luck had played a part, or that my wins were accidental. For a large chunk of my life I believed, wrongly, that other people were better than me (because they'd told me so), and in many ways my story and the lessons I've learned stand as a polar opposite to the type of narratives written by combat veterans, or fearless adventurers operating at the ends of the earth, all of them bulletproof to pain, fear or anxiety.

Eventually I learned that the limiting beliefs I had held about myself were wrong, my mindset having changed after taking up cave diving in the mid-nineties. I acquired the skills required to succeed and my attitude towards what was possible and what wasn't was transformed. As well as breaking those two cave-diving records, I also accepted a challenging role in which I helped to save lives as a volunteer for the South and Mid Wales Cave Rescue Team. It became my responsibility to locate and assist people trapped in horrific circumstances: individuals stranded in eerie, watery underworlds, detached from civilisation, and sometimes starving hungry, hypothermic and panicked. In many ways I had moved past what I thought was possible for a bloke like myself. And it is this ordinary-person perspective that runs through *Thirteen Lessons That Saved Thirteen Lives*.

Why is that view important? Because it shows that everyone has it in them to push past their limits while handling the type of pressurised situations or life events that they might have ordinarily shirked from. In many ways, I'm more Clark Kent than Superman. Think of me as an enabler for anyone trying to cope having been thrown into unexpected and definitely-not-normal circumstances, or as someone who has thrived under extreme pressure and emerged with a series of hard-learned lessons to share.

It is through experiences of this kind that *Thirteen Lessons That Saved Thirteen Lives* can, I hope, help anyone reading it.

When it came to rescuing those twelve kids and their coach in Tham Luang, the odds were stacked against them because many of the personnel sent to help – including the Thai Navy SEALs – had never been in a cave before. I had considerable caving experience, but unlike the team of elite military operators, I was ordinary. And yet I was able to locate and extract the Wild Boars. That was thanks to the challenges I'd experienced throughout my life, educational events that later proved to me that the first step towards any successful outcome was to respond positively to the Inner Critic that says, *'But you can't . . .'*

The next was to state, against the odds, *'I can.'*

Until, finally, it was possible to say, *'And I have.'*

By applying the processes detailed in *Thirteen Lessons That Saved Thirteen Lives*, everybody has the potential to rise up and succeed with their own challenges. As I've discovered, the results can be startling.

LESSON #1

START WITH *WHY NOT?*

The first steps are always the hardest, and all too often we're guilty of giving up on an idea because the end goal feels daunting. Even when the news had broken that twelve boys and a football coach were stranded in Tham Luang, I initially assumed that joining up with the rescue mission was an unlikely event. Not because the challenge of diving into the floodwaters was beyond me, but because I believed the difficulties of securing permission to work would be too great. It was only once I had asked the question, 'Why not?' and stopped thinking negatively that I was able to involve myself in the search and rescue mission. Without that one simple action, there's every chance the operation might not have been concluded so successfully . . .

DAY ONE
TUESDAY 26 JUNE 2018

The British newspaper headlines on 26 June 2018 made for bleak reading. Around a dozen kids from the Wild Boars football team and their coach were missing somewhere in the Tham Luang caves in Thailand. A storm had surged into the area, bringing with it an outbreak of heavy rain and the downpour had caused the tunnels in the caves to flood. Worse, nobody knew just how far into the mountains the group had travelled, and there was a real concern they might already have drowned. I scanned more and more news sites for any details about the search and rescue efforts. As somebody who had worked on such operations, I wanted to know who was on the ground and how they were functioning, and by the looks of things a mission was very much underway. Sadly, the weather conditions were worsening and there was speculation that a body recovery job might have to take place. I sighed. Whether they had survived or not, the work required to extract those kids was bound to be grim.

Thirty years of experience had taught me just as much. I had previously been asked to enter caves with the aim of bringing both the dead and the living to the surface, so I understood just how unpredictable the work in Thailand could be. My introduction to the sport of caving took place with the Scouts when I was a fourteen-year-old kid, exploring Swildon's Hole, a vast cave in the Mendip Hills, Somerset, that stands at around 9,144 metres (30,000 feet) in length. When it was first announced we'd be exploring the interlinking tunnels that curved into the hillside I felt excited. I had heard the terrain made for a challenging adventure and was accessed via a ladder set alongside a 6-metre (20-foot) -high waterfall. When the time came to go inside, the descent of the ladder felt bloody agonising. I had a slight build back then, and my muscles ached and trembled as I clung onto the rungs. Even though I was attached to a safety harness, I needed every ounce of strength not to fall off.

Once beyond this obstacle, our group climbed up and down a vertical tunnel called The Greasy Chimney and across a flat slab of rock positioned just above the infamous Blue Pencil Passage. However, the most challenging obstacles were three ducks* called The Troubles. The water level inside each one had to be lowered laboriously with a bailout bucket, though this was only half the job. Once at the entrance, the explorer then had to inch their way through the darkness on their back, while 'kissing' the ceiling in order to access the diminishing air pocket above. Once inside, the water rose all around them. The environment was intimidating, but I loved the challenge. Every obstacle was a rush and each test furthered my love for exploration.

My interest was amplified when, at our furthest point underground, the instructor for the day spun us a very tall tale of the challenges of overcoming Sump Two – a 6-metre (20 foot) -long, water-filled passage. He then went on to explain how it was a daunting task, even for an experienced caver, and that a bunch of Scouts like us should forget it.

'Anyone hoping to get through needs to lay in the water for

---

* A duck is a submerged tunnel with a tiny airspace at the top.

twenty minutes first,' he said, 'That way they can adjust to the very cold temperatures. It's virtually impossible. There's no way I'm taking you in there . . .'

At first, I took his warnings as fact, but not for long. He'd clearly been exaggerating, and the more I heard about the techniques required to make it through Sump Two, the more I felt compelled to return one day.

'That sounds like a challenge,' I thought. 'I'd like to do that once I've picked up some more diving skills.'

Having accepted my return as inevitable, I eventually learned the techniques required to succeed. I loved caving and became obsessed with the idea of cave diving, too; physically I was able to manage the effort because I was into climbing and hiking with the Scouts. But most of all I enjoyed the assault-course nature of overcoming obstacles in and out of water. In many ways, caving served as a great leveller at a time when I was immature, both physically and mentally – suddenly I could do things that a lot of the other kids couldn't. It felt exciting and I continued the sport with the Venture Scouts and into my twenties. Still, when my trip to the much-hyped challenges of Swildon's Hole's second sump arrived twelve years later, it wasn't to be the death trap it had been made out to be – but it was no cakewalk either.

For the exploration, I had borrowed an old fish-bowl diving mask, the type worn by the famous explorer and conservationist Jacques Cousteau, and attached a light to the side. At that point in my life I had only really explored dry caves and this was the first time I'd ever felt like a real diver. In that regard, pulling my way through the dark, muddy water of Sump Two along a fixed rope would prove extremely committing, because this was a 'breath-hold' dive – I wasn't using a scuba tank – and the effort seemed loaded with risk. Nervously, I submerged, pulling frantically on the guide rope.

Those challenges I'd been warned about as a teenage Scout very quickly became apparent. The tunnel could only have been around 60 centimetres (2 feet) high and it was hard not to feel a little claustrophobic as I wriggled inside. I moved along the rope quickly, making an effort to conserve oxygen, but the work was intense – I had to ensure that every handhold was firm and purposeful. If I lost my grip at any point, I would quickly become disorientated and then I'd be in serious trouble.

Bang! Suddenly, my helmet cracked into a jagged outcrop in the roof, an obstacle known to divers familiar with Swildon's Hole. I'd been forewarned that the only way to push ahead at that point was to force myself further down into the silty water. With my breath running out, there was really no time to waste. I swam quickly, pulling myself through a small squeeze into the rock before rising up on the other side and emerging in a pocket of air. The manoeuvre was nerve-wracking. But able to stand in the waist-deep water and breathe, I realised I'd been presented with an obstacle that was apparently beyond me, and had succeeded. *I was beyond Sump Two.*

There was no way I planned on going any further. An even more remote part of the cave lay ahead and if I landed myself in any trouble between the second and third sumps, help would be a long time coming. But just as daunting was the effort required to get home, and I needed to repeat my nerve-wracking journey through the tunnel. I had struck against my psychological limits. Feeling as if there was very little choice in the matter, I turned around for the entrance.

My adventurous spirit was roused. I later climbed mountains

in the Alps and explored American peaks such as El Capitan, the largest rockface in the Yosemite Valley, where I was able to understand and rationalise risk. But as far as I was concerned, the real adventure could be found underground. Cave diving was exploration in the purest sense. *Why?* Well, when Neil Armstrong landed on the moon, a flight path from Florida to the Sea of Tranquility had been plotted by rocket scientists to take him there. Likewise, when Sir Edmund Hillary and Tenzing Norgay summited Everest for the first time in 1953, they only had to look up to know where to go, roughly. They still had to pass through the dangerous Khumbu Icefall and across the sheer rock wall that would later become known as the Hillary Step, but the end was visible throughout the expedition: *the very top.* Cave diving, on the other hand, felt like the final frontier, because there were no maps, coordinates or visible landmarks to guide an explorer as they swam. In fact, the only way to discover what was around a previously unseen corner, or beyond a sump, was to look. And taking a look meant moving into the dark, or through a tunnel that might lead to nowhere. But the rewards were undeniable. Floating into a part of the earth that had never been seen by another human felt like a true honour.

I also understood that calm thought was needed for a diver to function effectively, especially because the world in which he or she was operating in was similar, in terms of danger, to climbing into the Death Zone – the area above 8,000 metres (26,000 feet) on a mountain such as K2, where a lack of oxygen strains the major organs to such an extent that rational thought and logical movement can feel almost impossible. Underwater caverns are dark, claustrophobic and intimidating places. A lot of the time, a diver needs to think clearly in order to negotiate the tunnels and waterways ahead. The experience is sometimes disorientating, especially for anyone not familiar with the smothering environment of a submerged labyrinth, and that brings its own risks. A novice might panic in a confined space, run out of air and die, or overestimate their abilities and then find themselves trapped with no way of escaping.

At this point I should point out the difference between cave divers and dry cavers. A cave diver is someone who explores submerged tunnels and caverns, whereas a dry caver works their way through a cave system on foot – or on their backside or stomach, depending upon the terrain. Within the cave-diving scene there are generally two types of explorer. The first comes from a diving background. Their experience of moving underwater begins with deep-water diving or wreck diving, and exploring an underwater cave feels like a logical progression in an exciting sport.

The second type of cave diver comes from the opposite position. They are drawn to cave exploration rather than diving, and their interest hinges upon moving through a dark and mysterious world, some of which can only be accessed by diving into water. The diving is really a means to an end and the discovery of new passages is the aim. I'd very much bracket myself in the second category, though anyone thinking there is technically very little to separate the two groups should know that when cave diving became a recognised sport during the 1940s and 1950s, a number of open-water divers decided to join in. Many of them weren't up to it. After several grim deaths, the cave-diving community closed its ranks to anyone not experienced in caving. This attitude remains in place today in the UK, where dry-caving experience is seen as a pre-requisite for a cave dive.

Over time I developed a cool head under pressure, and once I became more familiar with the fundamentals of cave diving, I thrived. But I was also determined to progress quickly, and I worked to pass my basic open-water diving qualifications and learned how to swim underwater in glasses, which was something I had wrongly assumed was impossible. (I had bought a prescription mask. Beforehand I'd been fine when swimming, but without lenses I found it impossible at depth to read the cylinder contents gauges or dive computer.) Later, I was mentored by a number of more experienced cave divers from the Cave Diving Group, such as Duncan Price, until I had gained enough experience to embark on expeditions of my own. Before long I was exploring caves with friends and pushing past the point in an exploration where other divers had given up due to fear, fatigue, or inexperience. I had tapped into something that allowed me to go beyond the limitations I'd imagined for myself.

Swimming through the pitch-black environment was intimidating. While moving through a shoulder-width tunnel in churning, muddy water, the darkness ahead punctured by a triangle of torch light, it was possible for an inexperienced diver to feel overwhelmed, and staying mentally composed was often a constant battle for novices. But for some reason I was able to overcome those stresses. I found composure; I was able to relax, think and plan my way through a network of watery burrows, keeping my terror in check, pushing past any rational fears I might have felt, and swim deeper into a cave than previous explorers. Not that I was competitive or reckless; I liked working within my limits, and my talents were being noticed. When other people found themselves trapped and unable to extract themselves from a sticky situation, I was sometimes called in to help as part of a rescue team.

Cave rescue in the UK is organised into regional groups overseen by the British Cave Rescue Council. These teams maintain a list of active divers with the skills and nerve to assist in the event of a flooding or cave diving incident – a roll-call of individuals with the ability to extract anyone experiencing trouble in a flooded subterranean environment. It wasn't something I had taken any interest in before, and I certainly wasn't anywhere near the top of the list, but when two dry cavers found themselves cut off by floodwaters in Dan-yr-Ogof in South Wales in 2008, I was called into assist with the work. Alongside two others, I helped them to escape.

During that one incident, I learned that cave rescues really weren't glamorous at all. In fact, there were all manner of stresses and miserableness to overcome if a diver was to succeed. It also became clear that rescue dives tended to happen at the worst possible moments. Cavers usually weren't trapped during a warm, sunny day; they were often reported missing in the middle of the night when the rain was pissing down, and over several years, I was called into action on occasions when staying indoors with a film and a takeaway felt like a preferable way to spend an evening. Dan-yr-Ogof was my first taste of such an event. When our rescue team arrived on site, the cave had already fully flooded and the currents in the main passage were so strong it was impossible to swim against them. It was time to plan.

The best way forward, I realised, was to pull myself along the floor, dragging a line reel with me, all the while moving between eddies, or sheltering from the currents by positioning myself behind an underwater boulder. By the time I had reached the stranded cavers, it was clear the flood was subsiding and after diving a dry tube with hot drinks and food to their location, we waited for the waters to drop, swimming out as a group once a small airspace had appeared. My first rescue had been a good one, and it was certainly an interesting introduction to what I could expect in later events. But, weirdly, there was no overwhelming emotion afterwards. I was simply happy that I hadn't let the side down or dropped the ball. The same sense of relief and quiet satisfaction followed every successful rescue dive from then on. More than anything, that operation in Dan-yr-Ogof proved that I had it in me to meet the challenges of a rescue head-on. I had also made a difference in a very dangerous event. That realisation would pave the way for what was to come.

As my exploration dives became more complex and achieving the objective became increasingly difficult, it was clear that I had what I have often referred to as a good *hit rate*. If that sounds odd, let me elaborate: long and complex explorations have plenty of moving parts to consider, and a lot has to go right if a diver is to extend the known limits of a cave system. Whenever I made it to the end of a cave, or reached an intended target during a dive, I called that achievement a *hit*. During a dive, any number of completely valid reasons to turn around can present themselves, but I've found that I have often been able to solve them and continue safely onwards. (Though I would never criticise a diver for turning around at any point for any reason. I've named a failed dive as a *miss*, but that's disingenuous. Personal safety should always come first.)

In that respect, I've developed a good hit rate. And in a rescue situation what is really needed is a collective of divers with the experience and capabilities to start the job quickly: without too much faffing around they can arrive on site, understand what's required of them and achieve their targets first time, every time.

But that style of work can be gruelling and intense, and in those situations, I have found it easier to adopt a particularly dark sense of humour, rather than complaining or adopting a pessimistic position, which is often the quickest route to failure.

There were other factors that set divers such as myself apart from a lot of the others. The first was that I remained focused, not only on the job in hand, but on my own personal survival. Safety was my priority and I very much understood the importance of *not being a hero*. I had read countless tales of mountain climbers who had died because they were trying to save the life of another mountaineer, one that was actually beyond saving. In desperation, they spent too long working on a negative situation that couldn't be rectified until, eventually, they themselves succumbed to an unpleasant, altitude-related medical condition. While I felt incredibly comfortable underwater, I was also acutely aware of the margins for error and so I kept a keen sense of just how close to death I was during every rescue attempt or exploration.

The second factor hinged on efficiency. I was quick, able to move from sump to sump at speed without too much trouble, and I often configured my kit before a dive in such a way that it was possible to swim through an area of water before climbing out again and scrabbling over a series of boulders, or a waterfall, to make the next sump. For some divers, just the simple process of arranging their air cylinders and mask in those situations could prove time-consuming. I effectively managed to reduce those fiddly moments to twenty seconds or so, and I wasn't one for hanging about. All of those skills made me the perfect candidate to assist in the type of disaster that was unfolding in Tham Luang.

And yet there were doubts.

Recalling those hours when I first learned of the disaster, it seems weird that I didn't immediately imagine myself travelling to Thailand. I even remember thinking, 'Surely someone else will be there to fix the problem . . . *Why would they need me?*' But I was falling at the first hurdle and paying too much respect to my annoying inner critic. According to clinical psychologists, the part of our brain that imagines, perceives and anticipates tends to focus on negative thoughts of this kind. It says, '*You can't*' when often, you can. This then sets off an edgy, fight-or-flight response, as if the person is being externally threatened. Handily, I knew that to make progress I only had to shift my attitude into something a little more positive and I decided to look at the situation differently by asking myself the question: Well . . . *Why not?*

My first response was to talk to myself as I would to a mate, or a loved one who was facing up to a similar question. I reminded myself of my successes and achievements; I recalled the successful world record attempts and a string of rescue operations. Then I listed all my attributes as a cave diver until, eventually, it was hard to imagine anyone more qualified. I know that a statement of this kind might set me up as being a bit arrogant – and just the process of committing that idea down on paper in a book makes me cringe a little – but the more I considered what was happening in Tham Luang, the more I began to accept the idea that I needed to go.

But just as importantly, Rick Stanton had to come with me.

We were a team. And in many ways, the style in which I functioned, in and out of the water, chimed with Rick's. I didn't like to faff about; I was comfortable when problem-solving alone and happy taking responsibility for my actions. By accident, this attitude had been shaped during our first-ever cave dive together in Gough's Cave in 2002, alongside another diver called Andy

Stuart. Moving between sumps, I had made an error: I hadn't clipped my mask into my fins and as the three of us crossed a dry section of cave known as Bishop's Palace, it detached from its storage place and disappeared into a rift – a long, narrow hole in the cave floor. Not relishing the dive back of 140 metres (460 feet) to safety without a mask, I suggested that Rick or Andy shuttle back a replacement to me so I could swim to the entrance more easily. Rick fixed me with a stern glare.

'What would you do if we weren't here?' he said.

He had a point. If I had been on my own, I'd have had no choice but to swim out, mask or no mask, and I certainly wouldn't have considered creating a rescue scenario for such a simple mistake. I also realised that Rick wasn't refusing to help, but he was very much telling me to deal with the situation as best I could. Cautiously, I submerged and groped my way back to dive base, looking considerably more composed than I felt, or so I was told. At the time, I thought it might have been a test. However, I quickly came to realise that Rick's take was to assume that everyone else was as capable as him. I was simply expected to cope.

On a number of occasions, our dive team was expanded into a trio, and Rick had often explored alongside a diver from Yorkshire called Jason Mallinson, who would later join us in Thailand. Together they had explored a number of notable caves, such as the Emergence du Ressel in France and Chevé Cave in Mexico. More than most, the three of us seemed to possess an aptitude for bold, long-range dives. We happily shared projects, such as the exploration of Pozo Azul in Spain, and also rescue and body recoveries, including the 2011 retrieval of Artur Kozłowski, who had died in a cave in the west of Ireland. While working together, Rick and Jason had also been responsible for the 2004 rescue of six stranded British soldiers in the Alpazat cave system in Mexico.

The circumstances in Thailand seemed to be in our favour. When it came to rescuing the Wild Boars, I realised that the very nature of the environment in which those kids were trapped was strangely suited to our abilities. The cave in Tham Luang was made up of nine sumps that extended for 2.5 kilometres (1.5 miles), and negotiating it required a mixture of diving, plus extended periods of walking, crawling and climbing in the dry passages. There were tricky slopes to navigate and problems to solve. In many ways it felt similar to the type of assault courses found on a military training base and exactly the type of situation I had enjoyed exploring following on from my first experiences with caving as a kid. It seemed almost built for us.

While unpacking the pros and cons of going to Thailand, the only downside was the politics surrounding such an event. The relevant authorities hadn't yet considered contacting either Rick or myself, and past experience had taught me that we needed a formal invitation from an international agency such as INTERPOL or the Civil Contingencies Secretariat. So far, we had received no such request, though we knew that Vernon 'Vern' Unsworth, a British expat caver, was assisting with the search and had suggested our presence, I still sensed that we would need take responsibility for securing an official invite. My proactive mood increased further following a lunchtime run with a workmate.

'Look, I know this is going to sound really cocky, but I think I need to get to Thailand,' I said. 'I think Rick and I can help to save those kids . . .'

His response was encouraging. 'John, if you think you're the best people for the job, you should really make your case.'

I then called Rick. 'We should be proactive,' I said. 'If we don't make this happen today, we could lose another twenty-four hours. And who knows how long we have to save those kids?'

He agreed. Like me, Rick understood the benefits of conducting a rescue with an experienced cave-diving team in place. From what we were learning, the authorities at Tham Luang were relying on the services of the Thai Navy SEALs, and while they were undoubtedly an elite military force, their skills were better adapted to boarding drug boats and repelling hostile forces rather than conducting what looked like an extensive search and rescue mission. I also knew from experience that whenever a cave rescue was attempted *without* a team of specialists, the results could be dire.

Undoubtedly, one of the most famous examples of this had taken place in 1984 when an experienced diver called Peter Verhulsel had attempted to explore the Sterkfontein Caves, which are located just outside of Johannesburg. Once he had been declared lost, a team of police divers had taken it upon themselves to conduct the mission, all the while ignoring the offers of help from a team of local cave divers. When experts were finally allowed in several weeks later, it was too late. They discovered Verhulsel's corpse slumped on a bank. He had died from starvation and by the looks of things his last act had been to scrawl a message to his wife and mother in the sand around him.

'I love you Shirl and Ma.'

In Thailand, thirteen lives were at stake, and so more phone calls were made. We contacted Robert Harper, a veteran British caver from Somerset, who had become involved in cave exploration with the cave diving group in the 1980s. Rob also had an intimate knowledge of Tham Luang. Through the work of Vern Unsworth, two connections with the Thai authorities were established and before long the Ministry of Tourism had invited us into the country. Any doubts I'd had regarding our involvement in the job were put to one side. Following a meeting at work that afternoon, I emerged to a series of phone messages and texts informing me that our flights had been booked. I really had no idea what to expect, or what problems might land in our lap as we made our way towards Heathrow Airport. I only had a few hours to ready myself for Thailand, which wasn't ideal, but at least we were on our way – and all because I'd been able to answer one simple question.

Why not?

THE CONVEYOR BELT OF SUCCESS

I'm not a fan of arrogant proclamations of faith; I've never been one for telling people to 'smash' their physical limits without care or consideration because, as a cave diver, thinking in that way can lead to serious injury or death (as it can in any extreme environment). Instead, I have long favoured a more considered, step-by-step approach to exploration. Which is why, when I first heard about the Wild Boars predicament, I was initially reserved about offering my services. Then I asked, 'Why not?' And having considered my position as one of only a handful of divers with the experience of rescuing trapped individuals in such dangerous circumstances, there was really no choice in the matter. *We had to help.* By simply answering that one question I was able strip away any doubts I might have held about my ability, authority or reputation. Suddenly the decision to travel became a hell of a lot easier.

This is a process I've gone through in a number of situations in my life, where doubt initially threatened my chances of even starting a project, or taking the first step towards a particular goal. By flipping the narrative into something more positive, I have been able to transform my thinking and in many ways, the experience reminds me of stepping onto an airport travelator – the type that moves an airline passenger from one set of departure gates to another. By asking, 'Why not?' I've made a decision: *I'm committing to the task*. And I only need to stand on the conveyor belt to reach the next action, propelled forward to execute the smaller, simpler tasks as they present themselves. In my case, having made the call to Rick, I just had to wait until a decision was made and the flights were booked. Then I was on my way.

The question 'why not?' however must be used in conjunction with the lessons that follow. It isn't an excuse to steam in gung-ho. A great way of visualising how the travelator process works would be to consider the first January exercise session after a heavy Christmas spent eating *all* the chocolates and drinking *all* the wine. By the first Monday of a new year, most people have become accustomed to long lie-ins and lazy days in front of the telly. Our bodies feel lazy and the thought of signing up to a gym class is unappealing. But when stuck in a mindset of that kind, the first step towards moving our bodies has to begin at home rather than on the treadmill. For example, our opening action could be as simple as putting on our kit and trainers. Psychologically, we've then committed to the task, and the strides that follow, though rough, suddenly feel like an inevitable progression. We shove a protein bar and a bottle of water into the bag. We then imagine our post-workout dinner. And by the time we're warming up or lifting the first dumbbell, we're much closer to completing the job than had been at the start of the day.

This idea was truly underscored in 2010 when I broke the world record for the longest cave penetration dive (categorised as the distance from surface) in Pozo Azul, alongside Rick, Jason and René Houben. When we first set out to explore the tunnels, my only ambition had been exactly that – *to explore*. There had been no great plan to set a record. In fact, at the very beginning all I could do was take my first step on the travelator because the thought of even exploring such a significant cave felt daunting.

To make that first step, I trained my attention on the simplest of early tasks, which entailed packing the appropriate kit, because that seemed like a manageable action. Having done so successfully, I'd boarded the travelator and effectively bought myself a pass for the next round of tasks, which involved driving to Spain, setting up camp and fettling* equipment in order to dive. But until that moment came, I only had to consider the first phase. Worrying about any potential hiccups or events further down the line would only have caused me stress and I instead adopted an attitude similar to the one of a (very) casual tourist whose only serious requirements when getting to the airport are their passport, phone and credit card, because those three vital items often represent the minimum inventory needed to travel. (For example, when going on holiday, if the casual tourist forgets to pack their sunscreen or swimming shorts, they can simply buy a new pair. I'd like to point out that my packing list for explorations was much, much longer.)

As with my first diving accomplishments in Swildon's Hole, my achievement in Pozo Azul helped me to accept that success

---

* A cave-diving term meaning to prepare

did not necessarily belong solely to those who believed in themselves fully. To reach an end target, I just had to commit to the first step: *to step onto the travelator*. And even if it seems hard to accept an overall goal, like the 10k race, or a dream job, it doesn't matter. By taking on the smaller tasks that follow, piece by piece, the conveyor belt does the work for us. We only have to keep up, one job at a time with the required tasks as they present themselves. *The 10k runner has to stick to an effective training plan. The job hopeful has to research the specifications of their dream role and prepare a CV accordingly.* The same process kicked into place as I stepped on the travelator towards Thailand. I made speculative phone calls, Rick did the same, until eventually we were moving towards our ultimate goal.

It wasn't long before I was packing my equipment for a flight to Thailand. The rescue was on.

START WITH *WHY NOT?*: THE CHECKLIST

- Think positive. Reframe the question.
- Remember your talents. Ignore the Inner Critic.
- Take your first step. Board the travelator.

LESSON #2

LISTEN TO THE QUIET VOICE

Cave exploration is sometimes about failure, but in a good way, and I can feel strangely satisfied whenever an obstacle or an uncertain situation has convinced me to turn around. For example, I've almost been to the end of many caves, but during a moment of high risk I have happily made the decision to end the exploration rather than push on regardless. The biggest upside of that attitude is that I'm still alive, but knowing exactly when to stop is a skill we can all apply to our everyday lives. (How often do you hear about projects where an investor has chucked good money after bad?) To do so, we need to recognise our personal warning signs, and one of these is the Quiet Voice, an internal whisper that sounds whenever trouble begins . . .

DAY TWO
WEDNESDAY 27 JUNE 2018

Chaos and unwanted attention dogged us throughout our journey to Thailand, almost from the minute we arrived at Heathrow Airport. Being rushed on to the flight by a British Transport Police escort was an early sign of the craziness to come. The plane's captain then needed to check on our diving cylinders and the equipment we were transiting to Thailand – *was it the sort of kit that could go bang and blow up the plane?*

Airline staff wanted selfies; crowds of people at Bangkok's Suvarnabhumi Airport wanted selfies, too; and once Rick, Rob and I had arrived at Chiang Rai Airport, we were mobbed by well-wishers. One group even approached us with a large banner. Printed on the front in bold lettering was 'The World's Best Cave Divers', which was a kind gesture, but the fanfare felt excruciating.

'How the hell do we get out of this?' I thought, as the three of us retreated into the shadows for what quickly became a forced group photo.

Not being one for big displays of bravado, I hated the thought of over-promising positive results. Given the way in which caves could flood and people often panicked, I knew that a search and rescue operation of the kind we were undertaking sometimes transformed into body recovery efforts. When we first decided to make the journey, it had been agreed that the best approach was to make a low-key arrival, but that was now impossible given that the global media's gaze was fixed upon Tham Luang and the compelling story of thirteen people stuck inside. Anyone arriving to help was being treated to a heroes' welcome, whether they liked it or not.

But while the public's support for our arrival had been overwhelmingly positive, the reaction from the local authorities felt resistant. Having extricated ourselves from the airport crowds, Rob, Rick and I were ushered into a private lounge where we were introduced to Mr Narongsak Osatanakorn, the governor of Chiang Rai province. As we spoke, the mood seemed tense.

'I'm not sure you can help,' he said, sternly.

Mr Narongsak looked exhausted. His tone also suggested he didn't fancy our chances very much, but his grumpy disposition was understandable: the situation in Tham Luang had worsened considerably over the past twenty-four hours. The heavy rainstorm was showing no signs of relenting and the cave's floodwaters were rising so drastically that the military forces tasked with finding the Wild Boars had been pushed back to the entrance. There was even talk of drilling a 'narrow shaft' into the mountain as an alternative entry point. It all seemed a bit desperate.

Elsewhere, the public mood had become increasingly frantic, which explained the slightly hysterical reaction to our arrival. As of yet, there was very little indication that the boys were still alive, but there were one or two reasons to remain optimistic. According to eyewitness accounts, the group had been spotted carrying torches as they entered the cave, which was a relief – there was some hope that the boys might be able to find their way to a safe spot in the dark cave. Their living conditions would be survivable, too: the temperatures inside Tham Luang were estimated to be somewhere between 20°C and 25°C degrees (though it would be cold if they were actually in the water) and there was plenty of oxygen to breathe, provided the boys had found a space above the waterline in which to wait. As long as nobody had been seriously injured, the Wild Boars had a fighting chance of survival.

Still, I understood Mr Narongsak's confusion at our appearance – as far as he was concerned, the rescue mission was already in the safest possible hands, since the Thai Navy SEALs had been called in to assist. Physically at least, they were unbeatable, though they had unsuccessfully battled the rising water for several days. We diplomatically pointed out that cave divers often employed very different tactics to those used by the military, especially during rescue missions. I then explained our track record when extracting people trapped in the type of circumstances being endured by the Wild Boars. Apparently our friend, Vern Unsworth, who was assisting the rescue effort, had emphasised our credentials too.

'John Volanthen, Rick Stanton and Rob Harper . . . these are the best cave divers in the world,' he'd said. 'Get them on the phone and get them over here.'

I worried that Vern's appraisal might have put a few noses out of joint.

Mr Narongsak went silent. Then he nodded.

Was he going to let us in? I really wasn't sure.

'Yes, you can help us,' he said huffily, though his gruff mood had made it clear our support was being treated as a nuisance. Hoping to assure him that we were every bit as competent as Vern had suggested, I grabbed the blue folder I always carried with me for rescue missions – partly to look official, but also to tick off a checklist of vital requirements that needed considera-tion before any type of work could get underway. Most of the info contained inside was basic stuff; the type of intelligence required by any crew operating in an emergency situation where time was limited, but I needed one or two extra details before we could start work, namely . . .

Do any of the kids have any pre-existing medical conditions?

Mr Narongsak looked back at me blankly. There was a shrug from the military aide sitting alongside him. Apparently, no such information had been gathered on the kids, which seemed a little strange given it was bound to influence how we extracted them from a very dark, very wet and very dangerous cave. If one of them was asthmatic, or suffered from a condition that might require us to take medication inside, we needed to know. I pressed ahead . . .

What's the detailed weather forecast for the next twenty-four hours?

The same aide reached into his pocket. '*Thank god*,' I thought. 'A detailed report.'

He then pulled out a smartphone and swiped through to the weather app. I couldn't believe it. The weather systems heading into the area was one of the most pressing issues to consider. Not to have an exact understanding of what was coming felt bloody worrying, though it didn't take a genius to work out that we were expecting plenty more rain.

'This is useless,' I said to Rick, making sure to whisper. 'They've not got any of the info we need . . .'

And when we later arrived at the mouth of Tham Luang and met with Vern, the dark maw was surrounded by the chaotic bustle of workers, military guards, police attention and media. It was hard not to get the sense that our arrival was nothing more than an unwelcome distraction. That nagging unease increased further as we prepared to dive for the first time, and after filling several air cylinders, our entry to the cave was blocked off by a severe looking Thai Navy SEAL.

'You can't go in,' he said, putting up a hand.

I sighed. Having worked on a number of high-profile rescues, I had become familiar with the chains of command that are quickly established by both military and emergency services. At most rescue sites there is often a process to stick to and procedures to follow, and as far as I was concerned it was important to bring some semblance of order and strategy to what could otherwise be an overly chaotic situation, especially if concerned relatives and journalists were milling around. In this case, the poor SEAL was only doing his job. But it felt like madness.

'Don't you know there are kids in there?' I snapped angrily.

With hindsight, I'd gone over the top and my reaction only ramped up the tension.

'I can't make the decision,' said the SEAL wearily.

'So who can?' I asked.

'Let them go in,' crackled a voice on the SEAL's walkie-talkie eventually. 'But tell them we're not going to recover their bodies if they die.'

Shaking off the hostilities, we stepped into the cave.

■ ■ ■

The water rushing through the mountain and into the Tham Luang caves was rising quickly – too quickly for my liking. As I moved forward alongside Rick and Rob, all of us loaded down with heavy diving kit and several air cylinders that weighed around 20 kilos (45 pounds), it was clear the first chamber had previously been set up as a show cave, an impressive space that was about 20 or 30 metres (65 to 100 feet) wide and the type of sightseeing attraction backpackers and tourists often found themselves visiting as part of a group excursion. The appeal was obvious. Huge, jagged stalactites dangled from the ceiling and a large spooky-looking passage disappeared into the darkness. The Wild Boars had explored these tunnels just a few days earlier, but who knew where they were? And then I caught sight of a chilling monument to the missing. Still chained to a wooden handrail at the cave's entrance were a number of bicycles – *the boys' bicycles*.

We made our way into the inky blackness of Tham Luang with a guideline. After a few hundred metres of walking and crawling, Rick and I clambered down a slope to reach a low point in the cave. Our view from the bottom was not encouraging. The threshing storm outside had intensified and the floodwaters, even at this early stage, were already waist deep. Worse, more and more rain was pouring in. I could see water bubbling up from below; it was running through a number of cracks in the rock, too. What was now a muddy lake was rising before our eyes, centimetre by centimetre. One, then two, then three. . . *How long did we have before this chamber was flooded too?* We had to move fast if we were to lay any more rope into the cavern.

Though we had only been in Thailand for several hours, I felt fairly comfortable at the thought of hitting the ground running. On previous explorations, my enthusiasm and Rick's more cautious approach had made for a good balance. (Though I'd like to point out I'm not gung-ho.) Once again, I believed that certain gains could be made by moving quickly, rather than hanging back and waiting. At the very least, the three of us might develop a clearer idea of what we were up against. That would give us a head start when it came to moving even deeper into Tham Luang the next morning. The surging floodwater had changed all that, though. On the way in, Vern had mentioned that the entire entrance was likely to be drowned in a matter of hours, but given the heavy rainfall, that now seemed a conservative estimate.

Then Rick grabbed my arm. He was pointing to a small, triangular passage up ahead. Moments earlier an air pocket of less than 1 metre (2 or 3 feet) had been clearly visible between the water's surface and the ceiling. Worryingly, that had now diminished to no more than 30 centimetres (12 inches). Worse, Rob had waded steadily into the darkness.

'The tunnel Rob's heading into is filling up too quickly,' shouted Rick as the water rose. 'It'll be fully flooded in no time.'

I took a pause to figure out our best course of action. In many ways, it would have been very easy to join Rob as he pushed even deeper into the cave, rather than calling time on our first search attempt. We had the right equipment and the experience to handle the situation, for sure. But given the unusual circumstances, and the thought of those kids trapped somewhere ahead, I realised our emotions had been amplified, and in situations where there was an emotional urge to move quickly, there was also a chance that we might find ourselves carried along by events rather than taking control of them for ourselves. Experience had taught me that rescues could sometimes spiral out of control for that very reason. To make a rash act in such a highly charged moment would only have increased the probability of something going badly wrong. The key to avoiding such a mistake was to recognise when to call time.

When detailing the risks attached to cave diving, I've often referred to The Incident Pit Theory – an explanation of how one or two innocuous happenings can lead to disaster. In many ways, it's like a domino effect, and according to the Cave Diving Group, The Incident Pit Theory is 'a term used by divers (as well as engineers and doctors) to describe how things can go from bad to worse with sometimes fatal consequences, without any of the incidents in themselves being high risk.' In diagrams used to explain this idea, the slope on the edge of the incident pit is always fairly shallow. I suppose it most resembles the end of a trombone. But with each poorly thought-out decision, the incident pit becomes steeper, until a crash to the very bottom becomes unavoidable.

In cave diving, this process can begin with the most innocuous of events: a diver might have slept poorly the night before an exploration and, feeling fatigued, he decides to enter a cave that is rapidly filling with water – *as we had done in Tham Luang*. With every mistake thereafter, the slope steepens. The rising pool churns sediment and sand, reducing visibility for anyone swimming underwater. At this point, the incident pit is still shallow enough to escape, but eventually, without the foresight to backtrack, the diver's position on the gradient becomes so severe that the cave becomes a death trap. After a series of poor choices, the diver is then unable to retrace the route back and becomes trapped in a watery tomb. This might sound extreme, but in activities such as cave diving, or high-altitude mountain climbing, the margins dividing success from failure, or between survival and death, can be small. The trick is to recognise the problems as they arise; if those problems can't be solved it makes sense to turn around.

As Rob waded forward, his waist and chest submerging, something told me we were heading into trouble, a little voice that said, '*You're edging into the pit.*'

I yelled out, sensing an early disaster, but at first my voice couldn't be heard over the in rushing water. Then I got louder.

'Come back!' I shouted.

Rob glanced over, confused. 'What's happening?'

When I looked across to the nearby triangular passage for reference again, it was clear our time had run out. There only seemed to be around 15 centimetres (6 inches) of air left. Thankfully – *finally* – Rob noticed the troubling surge behind him. He twisted and hopped towards us in the water, gulping air from what was left in the pocket above by tipping his head backwards. As we walked back to the cave's entrance, none of us were in any doubts about the challenges ahead. Rescuing those kids would require a monumental effort and time was very much against us. But turning around had been for the very best. To have pressed forward would only have invited disaster.

RECOGNISE THE WARNING SIGNS

In the early stages it can be hard to spot that you're actually circling the incident pit, probably because the edges are shallow and the first few steps can seem inconsequential – a forgotten front door key, an uncharged phone or a missed email. But as the gradient steepens and trouble looms, one or two indicators of approaching danger will often present themselves. The trick is to address these before they combine and the the incident pit steepens. I've learned in diving that it is much easier to take a step away early on, or while wading in the shallows where the act of problem-solving is unlikely to be hampered by real-time risks such as a limited air supply, poor visibility or even injury.

But as the problems mount, an escape can become increasingly difficult.

This reality also applies to everyday life: if we pay attention to the early and often subtle signs, correcting each problem as it arises, there's every chance we'll be OK in whatever it is we're doing. The key to avoiding the incident pit is learning how to recognise those worrying cues. For example, my 'tell' usually begins with a nagging doubt, the sense that something has gone wrong. Rather than dwelling on what my subconscious might be saying, I'll press ahead regardless. But once I've reassured myself with a simple sentence, one that's familiar to us all, and in a quiet voice . . . *I'll know*.

'It'll be alright.'

It'll be alright. I wonder how many disastrous incidents have started with those three little words? We might sign a business contract in haste, telling ourselves, *'It'll be alright.'* Suddenly, something in the small print financially impacts us in ways we couldn't have predicted. Or maybe a series of risky corner cuts during a house-building project results in some disastrous and costly structural damage. At first, getting away with it might have seemed easy. We told ourselves: 'Well, what's the worst that can happen . . . ? *It'll be alright.'* But suddenly everything *isn't* alright. We're in trouble and sliding deeper and deeper into the incident pit. If we're really unlucky, the slope might prove too steep to come back from.

Through self-awareness, I've mentally reframed that one sentence – *it'll be alright* – so it has become a hazard light, a personal indicator that tells me when I'm going too far and when to stop. As a result I'd like to think I have been able to pull myself back from the brink of misfortune on more than one occasion. But that's not to say that calling time in the shallows can be easy. In fact, it sometimes feels like an unnecessary delay in the moment, especially when so many motivational phrases urge us to throw caution to the wind.

No guts, no glory.

Fortune favours the brave.

Courage above fear.

It often requires more guts to turn around than to press ahead.

Understanding the importance of stopping is one thing. Knowing exactly *when* to pump the brakes is another matter altogether. Throughout my career as a diver I've certainly tended to err on the side of caution and I have often applied what I call the Joey Approach – an idea loosely based on the character from the 1990s TV show *Friends*. During one episode, Joey angrily accuses his housemate, Chandler, of overstepping a line in their relationship. In fact, Chandler has gone so far that the line in question is nothing more than a dot in the distance. Within the context of the show the gag was certainly funny, but I have since used that jokey concept as a cautionary reminder when cave diving: the only way to know that a safety line isn't about to be crossed is to stay so far away that it is nothing more than a dot.

In many ways, I consider every dive as I would the braking distances of the car I am driving. In that respect, the important factors to take into account are: 1) the car's braking ability; 2) the environmental factors in play, such as rain or ice; and 3) my mental alertness at the time, and whether I'm tired, distracted or under stress. I know that these three details will affect my safety if I have to screech to a halt suddenly, in much the same way that my air supply, the type of cave I'm exploring and my stamina will affect my performance when working underwater. By assessing those three factors, I can estimate how much of a buffer I have between myself and serious trouble.

This concept works across the board. For example, when starting a business for the first time, it's very easy to get carried away by optimistic cash-flow projections and appealing partnerships. An individual or team, excited by their progress, might take on deal after deal without really considering the workload. If they are not careful they'll become of a victim of their own success and find themselves overloaded with commitments and pressurised by deadlines. In those situations it's easy for standards to slip, leaving clients frustrated and and eager to take their orders elsewhere. However, if the same business can remember the line in the sand, if they can understand when to say no, they will be much more able to find the balance between production and cash flow, while still keeping quality high.

MANAGING EMOTIONAL TURBULENCE

The consequences of calling time on a doomed project can be emotionally challenging. It might be that we have invested a fair chunk of money into a business idea that has failed to live up to our financial expectations. Looking to resolve the situation, we take a bank loan and spend the money promoting the company in some way, or we attempt to inject a renewed sense of optimism into our workforce by upgrading the systems and practices in place. But aren't we just chucking good money after bad? A strong poker player understands the value in throwing away a pair of pocket aces when the cards on the table haven't gone their way. But he or she is fortunate: with the turn of another card they will know at once if their bold move has played out. *They are able to appreciate the benefits of their decision immediately.*

In most cases, however, rapid resolutions of this kind don't really happen. Having made the decision to scrap a project, or idea, we rarely get to see the suspected disaster impacting upon our lives. Instead, we then focus on the positives that might have slipped away rather than what could have gone wrong. Our regrets at stopping, unsure of whether success was really in our grasp all along, can haunt us for the rest of our lives. The trick is to write off those events as lessons, rather than failures. From there we can learn and grow, ready to start again.

Sure, in Tham Luang, Rob, Rick and I *could* have pressed ahead, and in the hours after our turnaround there was perhaps some concern that we had lost vital time, even though the consequences for wading deeper into the cave might have been terrible. Rather than breathing a sigh of relief, we were left with the morale-crushing sense of, '*What if . . .?*'

I remember previously experiencing this sensation keenly when attempting to retrieve the corpses of two divers stranded in the Plura cave system in Mo i Rana, Norway, an area known as the 'Cave Capital of Scandinavia.' The tunnels first formed when an underground river worked its way through the limestone in a valley located just a few kilometres south of the Arctic Circle. The cave itself resurged* in a beautiful pool, but in winter, the

---

* A resurgence is a caving term for a very large spring. Think of it this way: when it rains, the precipitation enters the top of a hill or mountain through cracks and crevices in the ground. Some of these cracks might be tiny or buried beneath mud. Others could be big enough for a human to walk into. That water flows through the hill, driven by gravity, and eventually emerges, or resurges, at the bottom, having made its journey through a series of cave passages. These springs are often the start of above-ground rivers. For example, Wookey Hole forms the head of the River Axe.

surface of the lake was known to freeze over regularly. Using a chainsaw to create an access hole was the best way in for any divers wanting to reach the waterways below.

The environment in the Plura was a nightmare to work in. To reach the bodies, Rick, Jason Mallinson and I needed to dive down to 120 metres (400 feet). To reach that depth and still have the time for any useful work, we needed to use rebreathers. However, in cold water, their ability to remove exhaled carbon dioxide is reduced, potentially leaving the diver short of breath. That physical reaction can lead to an increased sense of panic at best. The worst-case scenario, as we would eventually discover, was what had happened to the divers we had been looking to recover.

Meanwhile, if I ripped or damaged my drysuit, the chances of my surviving for long would be slim. Water would seep into the holes and hypothermia would rapidly follow, leaving me with the desperate choice of surfacing too quickly and facing the bends*, or making some attempt to tough it out in the freezing waters. I'd previously experienced the pain associated with a small leak in my drysuit on a dive in icy temperatures. A valve had flexed slightly, opening up the tiniest of holes in the suit, and the water had felt like a knife slicing into my side. I knew that protecting my thermal underclothing would be critical if we were to retrieve the dead in the Plura.

After two dives, we eventually located the first victim. By the looks of things he had become jammed in a small squeeze, and though his arms were floating gently in the current like seaweed,

---

* A painful condition caused by gas bubbles forming in the circulatory system when a diver comes up too rapidly from depth.

his torso had become stuck fast. Grabbing onto a hand, I tried to yank him free, but his frame was impossible to shift. Pushing him the other way proved just as frustrating, and it became apparent that his equipment was bunched up like a fish barb on the reverse side of a small opening. For a brief moment, I considered cutting away his kit before realising it was out of the question – the process would require too much time and manpower. *So what was I going to do?* There didn't seem to be an easy way of dislodging the body, but I was determined to keep trying.

If I were to take a guess at how he had died, it was probably due to panic. The diver must have become stuck in what was a very small passage in the rock and he'd flapped. In doing so, his breathing had quickened, which had then locked him into a downward spiral. The poor guy must have died from asphyxiation and his dive buddy, stuck on the other side of the hole and unable to free him or move past, had probably gone the same way too. Of the other members of the dive party, two had surfaced safely, another was somehow able to force his way past his friends; the last had made the long and dangerous return trip, and through a lack of bottled gas had ascended too quickly. This diver picked up a nasty case of decompression sickness in the process. Overall, it had not been a good week for cave divers in Norway.

Body recovery is important and I'm a great believer in closure – as a concept and a coping mechanism. It's important that a deceased diver and their loved ones can be reunited, albeit posthumously, and though their lives have been devastated by tragedy, there is some comfort in bringing a family member or friend to the surface for a decent send-off. Afterwards, the healing can begin and sometimes a tangible part of the process is for the family to meet the divers to show their gratitude for the effort. During our first body recovery missions, Rick was more comfortable in meeting with the bereaved, given his day job as a firefighter. But I gradually grew into it, understanding how important it was to the relatives.

Despite this moral obligation, I'm also aware that there is a limit to the risks someone should make in order to recover the already dead. Still pushing and pulling at the stuck diver, I checked my oxygen again. There was enough gas in the tank to make the surface, but only if my return journey ran smoothly – *and what was the guarantee of that in such treacherous conditions?*

'I need to try,' I thought, making one last desperate attempt to free him.

And then I heard the little voice.

It'll be alright.

I checked my oxygen one more time and assessed my safety limits. *The line that had started as a distant dot was now rushing towards me.* Realising I had already gone past the agreed duration of my dive, I turned around and made for home, feeling conflicted. I hated the thought of leaving a body in the water. When Rick and Jason later swam down to take another look, they both confirmed my assessment: the risks associated with retrieving the two dead divers were too high: we weren't on a suicide mission. But for a while, I was pained by the decision to leave them down there. I felt frustrated. I even briefly wrestled with the idea of going back down for one more look the following day, but the Navy divers working alongside us convinced me otherwise. The conditions were too perilous.

I later learned that a small team of Finnish divers had been more successful than us and were able to cut the bodies free during a clandestine operation, eventually bringing them to the surface a few weeks after our attempts. The work didn't come without consequences, though. At least one of the divers suffered from the bends afterwards and had required a period of treatment in a recompression chamber. The realisation that we had emerged from our failed mission physically unscathed eased some of the psychological discomfort I felt in the aftermath. With twenty-twenty hindsight I could at least reassure myself that we had made the correct decision and that nobody had been hurt.

In many ways I had to take on a similar attitude following our disappointing first dive in Tham Luang, but it was tough, especially given the high stakes in play. As I tried to sleep in a cramped bedroom later that night, topping and tailing with Rick in a shared double bed (because that's all the authorities had given us for now), I felt a little despondent. Outside, the rain was coming down in stair rods. I listened to it crashing on the tin roof above us and thought gloomily about how the floodwaters had beaten us back, even though we had barely entered the caves. I had to snap out of it and instead train my attentions on what lay ahead – another dive, another opportunity. Somewhere in the depths of Tham Luang, beyond that flooded entrance were thirteen people. One or two of them might even be alive.

Somehow, we had to find a way to the boys.

LISTEN TO THE QUIET VOICE: THE CHECKLIST

- Listen for warnings. Learn your personal cues.
- Evaluate safety margins. Stay within your limits.
- Know when to stop. Lose a battle to win the war.

LESSON #3

ZOOM IN, ZOOM OUT

Every challenge requires a healthy sense of focus. I say 'healthy' because too much focus can bring danger. That might sound a bit odd, but I've come to realise that it's possible to become so fixated on completing a task underwater that problems and dangers can develop around me unseen and I can become unwittingly over-ocused. For the most part, I try my best to regard these peripheral issues as being important, while maintaining a flexible and open mindset. This is vital if I am to avoid missing cues for things that might throw me off course later because during cave rescues, events rarely unfold in the way you would expect . . .

DAY THREE
THURSDAY 28 JUNE 2018

The following morning, Rick and I prepared to dive into the waters at Tham Luang, but our attention was yanked this way and that. Journalists wanted interviews and hundreds of workers milled around the cave entrance, where they were performing all sorts of tasks – some ran electrical wires into the tunnels, others helped to pump water from the submerged caverns. Their daily efforts had so far sucked away hundreds of thousands of gallons, which was no mean feat. But really, it was a pointless effort: the torrential rain was pouring *millions* of gallons into the tunnels and so the work must have felt disheartening.

'This is monsoon season now,' said one engineer glumly. 'The rain won't stop for months.'

As I watched him working, it was hard not to think of the apocryphal waiter rearranging deckchairs on RMS *Titanic* before it sank to the bottom of the North Atlantic Ocean.

There were now many rescue teams operating on the ground: in addition to the Thai Navy SEALS, individuals from the US Air Force 353rd Special Ops Group had arrived to help. Divers from the Australian Federal Police and Australian Navy had turned up too, as well as divers from the Beijing Peaceland Foundation. Alongside Rob, Rick and myself, there were now twelve divers from places as far away as Britain, Canada, Australia, Denmark and Belgium, but few seemed keen to jump into the now treacherous waters rushing through Tham Luang.

Despite this expanded rescue force, it was still hard to believe the Wild Boars could survive, or that we could even help them. If any of the kids were in one piece, our chances of successfully pulling them through the sunken catacombs seemed slim at best – even less so given Tham Luang was still flooding. As I walked and waded through the cave towards the murky underworld for our first exploratory dive, it felt hard not to wonder what our options would be were the Wild Boars discovered alive. *Would we have to support them until the floodwaters had subsided enough for them to wade away? Or could we pull them through the caves somehow?* It really didn't bear thinking about.

I have long learned that flooded caves have moods – or, at least, the waters running through them do. Their temperament can change from day to day, depending on the weather and precipitation outside. During our first peek at Tham Luang the previous evening, the floodwaters had been rising steadily, but in a way that felt escapable. In the time since our last visit, the cave's mood had darkened considerably thanks to twelve hours of relentless rain. The entrance floor and some of the chambers beyond were now submerged to a considerable depth and the water inside them whirlpooled and frothed like the rapids of some ferocious river. Anyone wading through the churn was at risk of being swept away and smashed against the rocks or sucked underneath and drowned.

Swimming inside the initial pools and tunnels made for ugly work and we were forced to fight against heavy currents through what were now submerged sections of cave passage. Psychologically it was tough going, too. Beneath the thrash and roar of the flood, there was an ominous feel to our situation and my senses were on high alert whenever I moved under the surface. In the dull glow from my head torch I saw air bubbles spinning across the murk in jets. They cascaded through rocks, their fizz driving mud and sediment into the currents. The sandy floor below had been swept into a grid of sidewinding ribbons, the kind you might see shaped across a Saharan landscape by hot winds, and their contours told me exactly how the water was flowing. *But I could feel it too.* The current thrummed around me; its pressure pulsed against my body and washed violently around my face mask and ears.

We moved out of the flood between sumps, scrambling over jagged rock or along perilous, muddy banks so slippery it would have been quite easy to skid, lose footing and fall. I kept my mask on to save time – neither Rick nor I wanted to faff about with our kit while moving from land to water, water to land – but my mobility was limited by the heavy equipment strapped about me: lead weights in my belt that allowed me to submerge more easily; the air cylinders attached to my waist; I was also wearing a helmet, a hood and a dive mask. These were the tools I needed to survive underwater, but they made my life a lot more awkward when moving above it.

Despite the heavy graft, I often considered diving of this kind to be quite good fun. In many ways it most resembled an underwater playground where all sorts of obstacles and challenges had to be overcome in order to explore whatever lay ahead. This time though, we were working under heavy duress. *We had to find those kids.* Enjoying the experience of overcoming adversity was impossible as we passed Tham Luang's first two sumps. Also, acting quickly was imperative. Soon we arrived at the last of the line we had laid yesterday, before the tunnels were fully submerged, but this time we were able to continue into the third cavern. Large by any standard, the space was over 10 meters

(30 feet) high and 30 metres (100 feet) wide, and with my head just above the water, I saw a mud bank stretching up at a 45 degree angle into blackness. I took a look around in the dark, flashing my torch into the corners for any clue of the Wild Boars' movements. It didn't take a genius to notice that this space was flooding very quickly, too. *But of course it was.* And then coming towards us from the back of the cavern, I saw a light moving unsteadily.

Then another. And another. Until finally, four were visible.

We weren't alone.

They were people, and at first I imagined the impossible was happening. I called out to Rick.

'That can't be some of the kids, can it?'

My mind raced. *If so, where were the others?*

There was an air of confusion. *And how have they managed to get into this chamber in one piece?*

I knew the thought of their making it to this part of Tham Luang was wildly optimistic. Chamber three had been relatively dry a day or so previously, so if some of the Wild Boars *had* been holed up here, they could have walked away from Tham Luang relatively unscathed. I also knew that swimming to this point from somewhere deeper in the caves was impossible without breathing apparatus – the cave survey told us that these areas were fully submerged. The shapes drew nearer, and then I recognised the faces as adults, not children, workers from the team of hundreds that had been sent into the tunnels to pump water and lay electric cables.

One of them shouted out to us in broken English and their situation became clear: having been tasked with pumping out a section of the cave, they had decided to take a quick nap, unaware the rainfall outside was increasing. As they snoozed, torrents of water surged through the tunnels cutting off their exit route. Judging by their reaction to our arrival, they had assumed that we'd been sent to find them, but in reality, they had been lucky. No one had any idea of their predicament, and pinned inside Tham Luang without breathing apparatus, they were likely to drown within hours if something wasn't done to help. It was a miracle for them that we had showed up in time.

Our focus changed. Suddenly we had to rescue the rescuers, and there was little time to lose – the waters around us were rising rapidly and the chamber was likely to flood to the roof. Wanting to save the four engineers from an unpleasant end, we had to evacuate them somehow.

After a quick discussion, we agreed that we should dive them out in a relay system, Rick and I moving the workers one by one, from chamber to chamber until we had made it to the entrance. Neither Rick nor I spoke much Thai, but we were able to communicate our plan through a series of hand gestures, the finer details of which would have sounded crazy to anyone familiar with the safety procedures of cave diving: our aim was to each hook an engineer under an arm as we swam, dragging them through the water with us.

It was set to be tricky work. For our dive that day, we had both brought two regulators – the breathing apparatus a diver held in their mouth, which allowed them to inhale and exhale. We would provide each worker with our spares as they swam, connecting them to our gas tanks, which would at least allow them to breathe, but this would be no easy feat. The currents were still charging about us and our visibility, once submerged, would be next to zero in parts. Matters were made worse by our having only two masks between us and it was obvious that we'd have to give these to the engineers too. I felt fairly comfortable swimming without one, but none of the Thais had any experience of cave diving. Unsurprisingly, they seemed less than enthusiastic about the struggle ahead.

'We're going to have to manhandle everybody through the water,' I said. 'We'll have to keep your bodies moving, no matter how awkward it might feel, so don't be surprised if we accidentally bump you against a rock from time to time . . . '

This was set to be a traumatic experience for everyone involved; the effort to succeed required a serious amount of nerve. But after a quick practice run, everybody seemed primed to move.

And that's when the trouble began.

I noticed the Thai workers talking frantically among themselves. One of them then made the universal hand gesture for 'mobile phone' and pointed to the bank where they had appeared earlier. I knew at once what they were saying and my heart sank. Their expensive iPhones were on the bank. Even worse, they were now refusing to leave without them. It was mindboggling.

'But we need to get you out of here now!' I explained, my frustration rising.

The lead worker shook his head. I didn't need a translator to understand. *We're not coming with you unless you take our phones too.*

I seethed. This was an infuriating battle, and I could easily have insisted that the workers forget their phones and move quickly – their lives depended on it. Instead, I relented, having decided to keep the peace, and annoyed, I swam to the bank and scooped the gadgets into a bag that was strapped to my air cylinder. *The situation demanded that these engineers be my new focus.* We had wasted what might have been valuable hours. *But what other choice did I have?*

What followed resembled an underwater wrestling match as we moved everybody through the first flooded chamber. The workers kicked and thrashed as we submerged into the blackness. To move forward, I used one hand to pull myself along the line while the other held the belt and trousers of the poor bloke I was dragging through the dark. I had to keep him close. If he drifted away from me at any point, there was every chance the hose connecting him to my air cylinder would yank free and in the dark it would have been impossible to find him. Without his regulator, or an exit route, he would drown.

At first, most of them seemed quite happy to be manhandled. But as their confidence increased, one of the workers tried to swim ahead to safety. With every forward thrust, I was forced to grab on even tighter, desperately maintaining the connection between their bodies and the air supply while holding as tight a grip as possible on the line. I knew that if I lost contact with the guide rope at any point, reconnecting to my route home would be next to impossible. Somehow, we managed to shepherd the workers back through three separate flooded sections, before guiding them safely through the waist-high rapids to the entrance. But our success was bittersweet. We had saved four lives, but I now felt increasingly doubtful about our chances of finding and rescuing the Wild Boars. I turned to Rick and shared my doubts.

'We struggled to get these four blokes through thirty or forty metres of flooded tunnels,' I said. 'How are we going to get a football team of kids through a couple of kilometres?'

The thought chilled me to the bone.

WHY OVERFOCUS HAPPENS

Flexibility in thinking was required even to contemplate saving those stranded workers from their sticky predicament. In many ways, leaving them to fend for themselves as we continued our search – for a little while at least – would have seemed an entirely reasonable decision at the time, especially as the Wild Boars were supposed to be our main priority. But acting in such a way would have represented *overfocus* and, through experience, I was able to acknowledge the realities of our new situation. Part one: the engineers were in trouble. Part two: moving deeper into the cave would only have caused us to use more of our air supply – maybe too much – and we'd have reduced our chances of eventually moving the four men to safety on the way back. They would likely have drowned.

Overfocus happens during moments of challenge or pressure, when it's very easy to become so absorbed in a target or a goal, that we lose sight of the bigger picture developing around us. Our peripheral vision shuts off, like a horse wearing blinkers, and we are left unable to spot other problems developing away from our central goal or target. Psychologists have even proven that this mental fog can change how a person perceives what is happening in their immediate vicinity. The effects can be a little unnerving.

This blindness was proven in 1999 with 'the invisible gorilla test', following an experiment devised by Dr Daniel Simons and Dr Christopher Chabris. In what has since become a famous video, an audience was asked to study a short clip in which a group of kids played basketball. Anyone watching was then tasked with counting the number of times a player wearing white passed the ball. As the action started, it became very easy to overfocus on the action; so easy in fact, that large numbers of people failed to notice a woman dressed in a gorilla costume as he stepped casually into frame. This phenomenon had previously been named 'inattentional blindness' by American experimental psychologist, Irvin Rock and Arien Mack, and Dr Simons and Dr Chabris explained that it occurred when someone becomes so fixated on a task or a series of tasks – in this case, the counting of passes made by basketball players wearing white – that their attention to any other stimuli becomes cut off. It is not just our vision that becomes distracted, either. It can affect the way in which we listen, too.

Away from scientific experiments, inattentional blindness can happen in all manner of ways. For example, we're all familiar with the story of the career-minded individual who neglects their loved ones and familial responsibilities by regularly staying later in the office or working weekends. Their partner then complains of feeling lonely, or unappreciated. There are tiffs and disputes, and the kids get upset, meaning some serious effort is required if a sense of equilibrium is to be restored at home. The same thing can also happen to parents. An example might be that one kid in the family is extremely gifted in sport or music, and their talent requires them to be driven around the country to compete or perform. But in those situations, it's very easy for the other children in the household to feel neglected.

Then there are the faster-moving occurences during which we can suffer from inattentional blindness, when a dramatic event such as an accident or some shocking news causes us to over-focus. I was once on a long car journey with a friend of mine and as we drove along a country lane at a fairly steady speed, she suddenly slammed on the brakes without warning.

'I've got to get out,' she said.

The car screeched to a halt. My friend was clearly in a bit of a state. 'There's an injured bird on the side of the road.'

When I looked across, I noticed a bloody ball of feathers. The bird was limping to safety having been clipped by a passing car, and my friend was about to step into the road. Instinctively I reached over and grabbed the door handle, holding it tight. We were on a tight bend; because of her inattentional blindness she'd lost sight of where she was. Any driver coming around the corner, even at a fairly slow speed, would have run her over, or careered into the back of our car. My friend had become so overfocused on saving the injured creature that she had forgotten her own wellbeing, and that of others.

Overfocus is acutely dangerous when cave diving, where oxygen consumption can feel like an overwhelming priority. While focusing intently on such a concern, it's possible to miss other vital cues or snippets of information that might suddenly prove important. For instance, if the air supply unexpectedly stops, an inexperienced diver will often focus only on their lack of air, grabbing for a spare regulator with both hands. But serious problems can occur if that diver then lets go of the guideline, or loses his or her bearings in the chaos. By rushing to solve one issue, they have actually created a far more problematic situation and they're suddenly lost in the cave. Instead, they should stay calm and swap their old regulator for a new one, all the while staying connected to their line. (In Lesson #5 I'll explain a process designed to stop stressful situations of this kind from spiralling out of control in the first place.)

But disorientation can happen so easily. When moving through caves, it's not uncommon to have to manage a great number of seemingly simple tasks or safety procedures all at once. Taken individually, these are usually unproblematic, but as they slowly mount up, it can become increasingly difficult to apply the appropriate amount of attention to all of them. The first of these issues is usually the guideline or, more pressingly, its exact whereabouts in the water. I always try to keep track of whether the line is to the left or the right of me as I move, as well as above or below, because if I accidently disconnect in the dark and need to grab hold again quickly, knowing its approximate position would at least give me some idea of where to move. That one matter alone can present a significant task.

Underwater, a diver's ears become a pain, too, sometimes literally, and it's important I make a concerted effort to clear them by holding my nose and forcing the air into my inner ear. Without that release, pressure can build, causing excruciating pain, and eardrums have been known to burst if these symptoms are left unchecked. Throughout a dive, a diver must also maintain neutral buoyancy, to avoid being too heavy and sticking to the floor, or too light and sticking to the ceiling. Their buoyancy must be adjusted as the depth changes and then during a dive as various air cylinders are used up. A diver might have four or five separate sources of buoyancy at any given time, including their drysuit, wing* and one or two rebreathers; and each rebreather must be constantly managed to ensure it can sustain life.

Then there is the issue of self-assessment. *How do I feel? Am I comfortable and in control?* When laying guideline through a cave, for example, keeping the reel under tension is always key – it

---

* A wing is a bladder of air worn on the back to allow a diver to adjust their buoyancy. With depth and weight changes, the diver can add or vent air from the wing, to maintain control.

stops the cord from drifting away too quickly. (And when that happens, a diver can be left floundering in the water, fighting coils of rope that will encircle them like a snake.) Also, when I dive, my tackle bag is usually attached to my body, so it's important I know what's happening there, too. So, all things considered, there is a lot to juggle and if ever those spinning plates come down, it can be very disorientating. In an overloaded moment, I've been known to check my air levels via the cylinder contents gauge. Then, having tried to recall the information, I have realised I hadn't absorbed the figures because I'd been too task-loaded and overfocused.

In 2004, I very nearly came to an ugly end in Wookey Hole – a mazy series of challenging limestone tunnels and caverns set in the Mendip Hills in Somerset. On previous dives, Rick and I had made it through the last squeeze*, beyond the known limit of the cave, which could be accessed with a little physical effort and a lot of nerve. At the time, we were around 70 metres (230 feet) underwater, but a large boulder was blocking what we hoped would be another small tunnel to the cave beyond.

I knew that applying a series of digging techniques at these depths hadn't been tried before, but we duly swam a crowbar, lump hammer and a lift bag† to the submerged end of the cave and began to attack the boulder blocking our path. We set upon the obstruction, first by using the crowbar. Then, with the help of our lift bag, we moved the boulder up and aside. A tight, body-sized entrance opened up. *And I was going in.*

---

* A small opening
† A large balloon made from highly durable material, which can be inflated underwater to offset the weight of items such as the boulder, allowing them to be moved more easily by hand.

For the best part of a week, I had been readying myself psychologically for this one moment. I sensed there was every chance that we might find a new tunnel behind that particular boulder, but I also knew it would take a fair amount of stress and risk to get there. After all, nobody had ventured as far into Wookey Hole before, so there was no telling what I was heading into and whether it might prove extremely dangerous. But the rewards were clear enough: by moving into this squeeze, we'd be able to continue the exploration and perhaps even surface or find a new dry cave beyond.

Focused solely on the undeniable rewards – the opportunity to extend a famous cavern, while recording a potential British record for the greatest depths recorded in a cave – I moved backwards, fins first, into the tiny gap. As I had practised in my mind many times over the previous week, I removed my chest-mounted rebreather and gripped the mouthpiece tight so I could inhale and exhale normally. I then dragged it behind me and entered slowly, face down, my mouth almost kissing the rock. For a few moments, this technique seemed to work quite well. I passed through the squeeze and into a virgin underwater passage, where the visibility was clear. The way on looked enticing.

Then disaster struck. As planned, I had not brought a guideline in with me for what was supposed to be a quick foray into an unexplored area, but as I turned around to make my exit, the world had darkened. A huge cloud of silt, stirred up by my movement, was billowing around me. I was floating inside a black hole, underneath a wall of hanging boulders, unsure of where I was and unable to spot my escape route back. An unnerving sense of panic started to rise. I had become so focused on not bottling it, that the reality of what might happen once I moved past the boulder had been overlooked. I had been distracted and as a result all the other issues in play had been forgotten.

I spun in the water, looking this way and that, hoping for some handle on my position and to spot any possible escape routes. *Would Rick know not to come in after me? Would he be sensible and wait it out?* I worked my way systematically along the boulder choke, looking for the hole I'd come through, taking care not to bring a wall of rocks down on top of me. Then, unexpectedly, *there!* I spotted a flicker of light in my peripheral vision. A torch was being flashed to my right, much further away than I had anticipated, and my fingers reached for the tunnel entrance I had dropped through just moments earlier. I realised instantly that Rick was trying to signal the way out without committing himself to entering the squeeze.

Pushing my rebreather in ahead, a pair of ghostly hands suddenly moved through the gloom, and I felt a tug. Rick had seen a flash of yellow from my equipment and was making a grab for it. He was now pulling me towards him into safety, through the gap between the boulders, my grip on the rebreather in my mouth. I clenched my jaw, not wanting it be yanked free in what felt like a grim game of high-stakes tug-of-war. The thought of choking on water in such a confined space was terrifying, I would definitely drown, but I was through in moments, floating serenely again in the passage, safely through the squeeze and contemplating both the swim out and the inevitable hours of cold decompression.

Our return was fairly uneventful, but the lesson had been clear: when working towards a target or goal, never lose sight of the peripheral detail. I had been bloody lucky in Wookey Hole.

BECOMING BLANKLY RECEPTIVE

So how do we avoid overfocus?

Before my experience in Wookey Hole, I had known that concentration is everything. Focus was incredibly important when exploring a claustrophobic tunnel where it wasn't uncommon to have to wriggle through a narrow, underwater gully with barely enough room to move my arms or legs. Sometimes it was impossible to see more than a few inches in front of my face because of the thick sediment churning around in the water. *Of course I was going to develop tunnel vision in those situations!* What I hadn't realised was that inattentional blindness could be so acute – and life threatening. That one incident taught me that I had to ensure my concentration was not to the detriment of whatever else was going on around me and that I had to avoid overfocus at all costs.

I soon came to understand that it was much better when working under pressure to sit back and maintain a wider view of a situation. I began practising a technique perfectly described by sci-fi novelist, Arthur C. Clarke in his 1982 book, *2010: Odyssey Two*, in which one fictional character, unsure of what he was really looking for, becomes 'blankly receptive' as he searches through a stack of documents. In doing so, he realises he's suddenly alive to all possibilities, opportunities and risks without becoming overly fixated upon just one. I decided to behave in the same way: whenever I was unsure of what events or issues were the most significant, I would act like the character in Clarke's novel. I'd try to be flexible and receptive – characteristics required on all manner of rescue operations. By using a series of reminders and cues, I eventually learned that it was possible to maintain that mentality, even when working under pressure.

My second day in Tham Luang illustrated this approach being flexible and receptive to switching focus prevented me from being thrown off course after finding those stranded workers in chamber three. Yes, I was supposed to be rescuing the Wild Boars, but having assessed the engineers' situation, we had to shift gears and swim them to safety. (I also made sure to observe and memorise the waterways and rock patterns so they would feel familiar on my next dive.) In a non-diving context, our aforementioned, overworked partner could avoid over-focus by taking time to check in with their loved one's emotional needs and wellbeing during what would have been a pressurised situation. And the parents forced to drive their prodigy of a son or daughter around at the weekends, should be mindful of the impact that might have on their relationship with the other siblings.

As many people discover to their cost, commitments of this kind are the first to be discarded when the pressure comes on, but in reality it's healthy to remember that the peripheral stuff can be equally as big a deal if left unchecked. During high-pressure events, becoming blankly receptive is a helpful tool because it provides context to our main focus. More importantly, it reduces the risk of being blindsided by a boulder-sized problem arriving from left field.

ZOOM IN, ZOOM OUT: THE CHECKLIST

- Look up and around. Watch the big picture.
- Avoid overfocus. Don't get fixated.
- Understand your capacity. Allocate awareness appropriately.

LESSON #4

REST AND DECOMPRESS

In diving terms, decompression is an important procedure. At depth, water exerts a pressure upon the body forcing the gases we breathe – including nitrogen and helium – to dissolve into the bloodstream. Surfacing too quickly can cause painful bubbles to form. At their worst, these bubbles can affect the tissues, joints and major organs in a reaction known as decompression sickness, or 'the bends'. To avoid this problem, a diver will slow their ascent, resting or 'decompressing' underwater at different depths on the way up, making a series of stops that can last minutes or hours depending on the length and depth of the dive. But decompression is a vital tool for all of us, whether through physical or mental rest. And a period of recuperation from whatever it is we might be doing can give us the space to recover, recharge and discover new perspectives . . .

DAYS FOUR, FIVE AND SIX
FRIDAY 29 JUNE – SUNDAY 1 JULY 2018

Setback after setback crashed into us like waves.

By morning, the conditions in Tham Luang had worsened considerably, and a series of large pumps at the entrance, installed to help draw water away from the more remote parts of the caves, had become overwhelmed by the rising flood, causing diesel to leak into the churning currents. Oily, unctuous liquid oozed everywhere and the taste of it caused my stomach to lurch as I swam towards the third sump once more. Rick seemed to be having a much worse time with the diesel than me and was visibly gagging, but as we pressed on regardless, I noticed a set of lights drifting towards us in the water. It was another diver; he seemed to be searching for a suitable place in which to surface, but he had overshot the nearest airspace. Reaching out, I grabbed at his body, dragging him up to safety. When his head broke water, I could see it was the Belgian, Ben Reymenants. He looked visibly rattled.

Ben had proved to be an interesting presence during our first few days in Tham Luang. A technical diving instructor working in south Thailand, he had acted as an enthusiastic self-publicist, advertising his arrival at the cave entrance with a slew of social media posts and announcements. Very early that morning, he'd entered the cave heavily loaded with kit, but the water around sump three was still moving rapidly; visibility was poor, and so travelling while weighed down with a drysuit, rebreather and all manner of technical equipment was a risky choice. My opinion of Ben was that he wasn't a great listener; we had also been warned that he sometimes overplayed his achievements. Clearly, he was struggling a little, and yet as we shouted over the noise of the rushing water around us, he claimed to have a laid over 100 metres (330 feet) of guideline before being pushed back.

Despite his protestations, I wasn't entirely convinced. The conditions in that part of the cave were still unmanageable, so to have laid such a length of line sounded fantastical at best. But as in fishing, it's not uncommon for cave divers to exaggerate the nature of their successes. Spend any time in the pub with cavers and anglers and you'll hear increasingly unbelievable tales of how a tunnel went on 'for miles', or how a wrestling match with a carp turned into a battle to resemble Captain Ahab's struggle against the infamous whale, Moby Dick. Ben had managed to lay some line before being turned around, but by our later estimates that amounted to just a few metres.

Rick and I felt the cave conditions were exceptionally dangerous and decided against trying any further progress. I was happy to turn around; we needed to let the waters subside, and continuing on felt like pushing our luck. The three of us waded and swam back through the muck and murk to the entrance. There, the mood among the rescue teams was becoming more and more gloomy. Swimming beyond the third cavern seemed unlikely to be possible, and that meant the odds of our finding and saving the Wild Boars were decreasing rapidly. The velocity of water surging through Tham Luang was just too powerful, and the conditions didn't look like improving any time soon. A day or two earlier, Vern had said darkly: 'When the monsoon starts, it doesn't stop for months.'

Meanwhile, the Thai Navy SEALs' reluctance to accept our assistance was hardly helping matters. Even though we had helped to extricate four Thai engineers from a potentially lethal situation, our tactical suggestions and requests for information and materials were being pretty much ignored. In all, it was hard not to feel pessimistic.

'It's not looking good, is it?' I said to Rick as we checked over our kit later that day.

He nodded sombrely. 'We're done, aren't we?'

To come to any other conclusion under those circumstances would have been a flight of fantasy.

Our acceptance that the Wild Boars were probably beyond saving increased when news was leaked of another bizarre incident in the cave. Apparently, three engineers working in the water had experienced epileptic fits – *at the exact same time*. But the story sounded too freakish to take at face value. A more likely, and more unnerving, explanation for the seizures was an electric shock. I shivered at the thought of what was a worrying web of criss-crossing wire and light bulbs dangling from the cave roof and clinging to the walls. Sure, they were doing a pretty good job of illuminating some of the darker nooks and crannies of Tham Luang, but the bulbs were also a horrific disaster in the making. The set-up had looked so precarious that twenty-four hours earlier I had even pointed out my concerns to an engineer.

'The lights are pretty close to the water. What's the deal?'

'Oh, no, they're *special bulbs*,' replied the engineer, enthusiastically.

'*Really*? They look like normal bayonet fittings to me, strung on bits of wire –'

'No, they're *special bulbs*,' he said again, clearly not in the mood for my concerns. 'The power trips if they get wet . . .'

I found it hard to share his blind faith in what looked like an oversized mesh of cheap fairy lights, but given he was a professional engineer I pressed ahead, hoping that the circuit-breakers in place would do their job. Clearly, I had been wrong. Those three 'epileptic' engineers were evidence that Tham Luang was fast coming to resemble a building site, and one that had been bolted together far too quickly for my liking. Every incident, plus those political pushbacks, now resembled a veiled warning: *it was time to leave.*

As Rick and I talked through the merits of staying, we learned the US Air Force were making plans to withdraw, which came as no surprise. When asked whether the kids were still alive, one senior US team member shook his head at me sadly.

'Not a chance,' he said.

Taking this as yet another sign, Rick mentioned our thoughts of heading home to the Thai authorities, who flatly squashed the suggestion. Their tone was one of disbelief, probably because they had realised that the sight of rescue teams packing up and leaving Tham Luang would only deliver a grim message to the watching world. *The kids are dead.* We were left with very little choice but to tough it out in what was becoming a very depressing environment, and the only rational way of maintaining an emotional even keel was to create a distraction. Which is probably why Vern decided to drive us to a nearby temple the following morning for what he promised would be a cultural adventure.

On the face of it, this sightseeing trip might have looked like an insensitive thing to do, given the circumstances, but really, we were all out of options. The visit also carried some connectivity to our work because the temple was located at a resurgence in Wat Tham Pla, just along the hillside from Tham Luang. Sadly, the rescue authorities were thinking of knocking it down. Their hope was that if enough water could be pumped from the caves via this route, the water levels inside might miraculously drop, or an alternative entry point to the kids would reveal itself.

Ordinarily, I'm not a lover of buildings; nature has always been more my thing. But as I stared at the ornate temple with its gold spires and stone domes, a gang of monkeys perched upon its balconies and turrets, I couldn't help but wonder if the rescue operation was going a bit *off-piste*. Just because a large amount of water was emerging at this one particular location, that didn't mean it was in any way connected to the tunnels where the Wild Boars were sheltering. In much the same way that pulling out the plug in a household sink won't do anything to drain the bath – the two units, though attached to the same plumbing, operate independently. Similarly, the network of passages draining water from the nearby Doi Nang Non mountains weren't necessarily linked and a chemical analysis of the water had proved as much. My hunch was that draining water from Wat Tham Pla, or any other resurgences along the base of the hill, would have little or no effect on Tham Luang. Destroying the temple seemed like a terrible, and probably pointless, effort.

But as we explored the site, and later drove to a nearby cave where massive pumping efforts were already underway, the visit took on a more transformative mood. The Wat Tham Pla temple was fast becoming a perfect distraction for the group and having worked, almost nonstop since arriving in Thailand, my body and mind were in desperate need of a break. The effort to dive deeper into the submerged caves, along with the politics outside it, had become so psychologically taxing, not to mention bloody knackering, that I had been pushed close to breaking point. Taking a brief rest from the grind delivered a restorative boost, and I felt both stronger and sharper after our morning away from the rescue.

In many ways I was reminded of another search operation I had been involved with in 2010, when the French caving expert and commercial diver, Eric Establie had been declared missing somewhere in the cave of the Dragonnière de Gaud, in the Ardèche Gorge. When the French authorities realised the depth and complexity of the cave, Rick and I were called in to help the rescue effort, but having arrived, it was hard not to be over-whelmed by the scale of the operation. The area was teeming with various members of the emergency services. Engineers and rescue workers busied themselves, all of them in place to assist our efforts. But as soon as I saw the incredible infrastructure in place, seem-ingly there to support us at the sharp end, the weight of responsibility piled on top of me, and I became unsettled. Walking alone into the nearby forest, I created a little psychological space for myself in order to recalibrate. I needed to give a quiet pep talk to convince myself that I was capable of the job ahead.

'You are the man,' I said, quietly. 'You can do this. *You are the man . . .*'

Despite this renewed sense of optimism, our efforts eventually proved fruitless. After a number of arduous dives during which we reached, but could not pass, a rock fall that had trapped Eric, the emphasis of the rescue changed. It was decided that we should have a day off while the others dived, and when our police liaison from the rescue team offered to take us to the top of Ardèche Gorge, we jumped at the chance. The view, when we arrived, was incredible. The rescue work that was going on had appeared impressive from the bottom of the valley where we had been diving. But from high up on the plateau, a completely separate and massive effort was underway – and it was on an altogether different scale. I watched police vehicles moving along the roads like little ants. On another plateau above the valley, demolition crews blasted their way through the limestone bedrock in an attempt to reach a vertical cave – one they hoped would lead to the stricken diver. What now looked like a small city was growing around a huge hole in the landscape.

The scene had a calming effect. Stepping back from the pressures of diving gave me a chance to find some fresh perspective and I realised that being too close to the action had created a sense that wasn't too dissimilar to sitting uncomfortably near to a TV: I could make out the shapes moving on the screen around me, but it felt impossible to pick out any clear detail. Stepping back and relaxing had widened my perspective, and I was able to still my mind. It didn't take long for me to realise that Rick and I were not alone in trying to locate Establie and I was able to calm a little for our next penetration into the cave.(Sadly, though we were able to locate Eric and bring some closure to his family, we had arrived too late to help. He had already passed away even before the alarm was raised.)

The same mood had settled upon me in Tham Luang. Not twenty-four hours after our visit to the temple, Rick and I were back at the cave, our diving kit in place, both of us feeling relatively optimistic about the situation – and with good reason. The waters that had held us back for so long were retreating. Some reports were even indicating that the chaotic currents that had blocked our progress, yanking us this way and that, had calmed a bit. With this new perspective, there was at least some hope. This sense of optimism was increased further with the help of both the US Air Force, and, unexpectedly, the Thai Navy.

Finally, they were allowing us to access the vast logistical resources at their command. The disparate organisations at Tham Luang were beginning to coalesce into a team.

We were going back in.

ENJOY THE SILENCE

True fact: I can fall asleep underwater. During periods of decompression*, while I'm waiting, submerged, in a cave, my body slowly adjusting (or 'off-gassing' as divers call it), from time to time I'll drift off. Partly, that comes from the fact that I feel very comfortable underwater; psychologically I am at ease with what might be considered by some people to be an almost alien environment. Mainly, though, I'm able to relax because I am cocooned away from the outside world. I have been self-employed for pretty much all of my life during a career in which I have run an IT company. That responsibility has meant that I am always at the mercy of the whims of clients and contractors. A phone call, or work emergency can strike at any minute. But underwater, I'm shielded from those distractions. While waiting for my body to adjust to the shifting pressure, there is often nothing else to do other than to relax. It can be very tranquil.

In fact, my only job under those circumstances is to avoid surfacing too quickly. To rush or cut corners might expose me to the painful and very dangerous side effects of the bends, and whether

---

* Decompression time can last anything up to a number of days. A diver must stop for certain lengths of time at specific depths during their return journey to the surface. These stops are calculated based on the combination of depth reached, time spent under water and gas mix breathed by the diver.

I'm required to hang around for five minutes or a number of hours, it really doesn't matter. During decompression I am forced to wait and relax. For all I know, the world might be burning outside the cave, but I wouldn't have a clue; even if I wanted to, there would be nothing I could about it do anyway. In many ways, it's a bit like being stuck on a long-haul flight. Once the 'Fasten Seat Belt' signs have flashed on, every passenger is expected to turn off their mobile phones and electronic devices. Unless you're one of those masochists who pay exorbitant fees for inflight WiFi, it is possible to enjoy a few hours of peace, uninterrupted by texts, calls or emails.

Underwater, my breathing naturally slows. I can feel my limbs floating around me. Apart from the sound of bubbles percolating from my mask and the gentle pulse of water in my ears, there is nothing to disturb the silence. Though I'm not an expert in enlightenment or the art of meditation, waiting and resting underwater has become an excellent way for me to connect with the present and to live in the moment. Decompression allows me to slow down my mind. After what will have often been a gruelling number of hours spent underwater or climbing over boulders while carrying heavy diving gear, the body, too, can take a well-earned break.

At times, it is also possible to eat and drink while hanging out in a submerged cave. One method for doing so involves a habitat – a contraption that creates a pocket of air for a cave diver to swim into for rest or food, and over the years, I've noticed that cave divers can be a creative lot. Habitats have been made from all sorts of unlikely items, such as upended wheelie bins or huge, repurposed chemical drums. Positioned upside down at the roof of an underwater cave, the air pressure inside pushes the plastic container upward, fixing it to the ceiling. Once it's positioned, a weary diver can move inside and safely relax in a pocket of air.

It is feasible to eat without the use of a habitat while diving, though it requires a certain amount of practice to ensure the regulator you are trying to breathe from doesn't get clogged up by any food particles. It's also possible to take things a little *too* far. During an exploration of the Doux de Coly cave in France in the early 2000s, the German lead diver, Michael Waldbrenner casually remarked to one of his support divers that he quite fancied 'a Big Mac and fries', such was his relaxed state. With over ten hours of decompression time to go, his teammate decided to show initiative and performed the 800-metre (875-yard) swim to the surface and back, plus a 50-kilometre (30-mile) round trip in the car, getting to and from the nearest golden arches in record time, and arriving back at the habitat with a waterproof bag containing the still warm meal. I'm not entirely sure how Waldbrenner was able to swim to the entrance afterwards. I certainly couldn't have faced the Big Mac, or the swim out, had I eaten it.

The point is this: it's vital that everybody finds the space and time for physical, mental and emotional recovery during tricky challenges or gruelling workloads, because rest and recovery is essential if you are to see a particularly tough job through to the end. Even the smallest of breaks can deliver a spark of inspiration, or a second wind, as I know only too well. I remember running in a painful, long-distance race in Greece that comprised 180 kilometres (112 miles) and concluded in Olympia. As I shuffled towards the top of a hill some 120 kilometres (75 miles in), my mind began to hallucinate. Exhausted, I was plunged into a deep despair. Eventually, I staggered towards a checkpoint, fearing my race was done; I was very close to the cut-off time and every muscle in my body wanted to quit. *If I could just rest, close my eyes . . .*

When they opened again, I realised I must have caught twenty minutes of sleep on the floor – for most of it I had shivered and drifted in and out of consciousness. Feeling slightly better, I drank a cup of coffee and then set off down the road, trembling in the cold. But as I forced myself to run, the world suddenly looked very different. The dark night had given way to a rising dawn, which glowed across the hills. I had more energy, and I eventually finished the race in a very respectable time of twenty-six hours. Often success comes down to a moment, or a series of moments, and how you act within them defines the whole enterprise. Taking a break, as I had done in that race, or performing some other action that might feel lazy, or unthinkable at the time, could actually be the right thing to do if it is an act of self-care – even a breather in an upturned wheelie bin can work.

Sadly, these days we are encouraged to push ourselves to our physical and psychological limits, usually in the pursuit of money or materialism. Our phones have shackled us to the office and often we are unable to escape the distraction of contract disputes, deadlines and office politics, even when we're relaxing on the sofa at night and watching telly. A burgeoning attention industry often hijacks our adrenal system with worrying headlines and 'Breaking News' banners that scroll across the bottom of our TV screens. These serve only to place us in a constant state of hyper-alertness. For much of our day, we operate in our fight-or-flight setting and the experience can be draining.

It is for this reason that learning how to switch off in order to rest and recuperate is a handy skill when facing up to tricky challenges. The idea that we cannot perform at our best when we're knackered is hardly revelatory, and yet so many people decide to ignore scientific and medical wisdom and attempt to execute difficult tasks while frazzled. People fall asleep at the wheel on motorways and die. Explorers push themselves to their limits and require rescuing. And business people – the type you might see competing on *The Apprentice* – eat poorly, party hard and break themselves in a stressful work environment. The emotional and physical effects can be debilitating.

But how can we know when to lift our foot from the pedal? Or to take a break when attempting to complete the perfect deal?

In cave diving, it's quite easy to spot the tell-tale signs of fatigue because the work can be so obviously taxing on the body. For example, when embarking on a long cave dive, I will often experience discomfort in my lower back. This is caused by the muscular tension that every cave diver experiences in the water when they're pushing against a series of strong currents, especially when transporting equipment or riding a scooter*. My jaw sometimes becomes painfully tight too – particularly when swimming in very cold water – and this discomfort is caused by clenching or biting down too hard on my rebreather mouthpiece. (Though not so hard that I might actually bite *through* it. That would be disastrous.)

Scrambling over rocks or along muddy banks can be equally challenging, and I am often required to move under a heavy load,

---

* A scooter is the James Bond-style propulsive device, or deep propulsive vehicle (DPV) that a diver uses to move through the water at speed.

which is brutal on my muscles and joints. It's not uncommon to be lugging around 50 kilograms (110 pounds) of equipment over ground, a load that comprises diving cylinders, rebreathers, mask, helmet and lights. Staggering under all that weight, especially when negotiating a slippery and uneven surface in the freezing cold is grinding work. My shoulders ache. My quads ache. My neck aches. Even my face can ache as a result of wearing a mask for hours on end. Making sharp decisions under pressure, and when in discomfort, is a pressing issue, so in those moments I like to think of myself as functioning within a state of *comfortable* discomfort. I relax into the misery, accept it and carry on.

It is when the pain and fatigue intensifies into *uncomfortable* discomfort that issues arise, and any negative incidents are usually triggered by desire. When things are going well in a cave dive, it's easy to look past physical and mental exhaustion in order to break a record, reach the end of a line, or explore a previously unseen tunnel. But this urge to push beyond a breaking point can be dangerous, because it is in these finely poised moments that mistakes are made – mistakes that can lead an individual to tumble into the incident pit, especially if they're knackered. The key is instead to relax and listen to the Quiet Voice once more (see above). When the pain becomes too much, or the brain begins to fog with exhaustion, I know it's time to make some attempt at rectifying the situation. But only once I've heard those famous last words.

It'll be alright.

I'll know that if I can't then fix the problem sharpish, it's time to head for home.

Most importantly, turning around when there is still plenty left in the tank means that the effort required to get going the next day shouldn't be as taxing as it would have been had I worked myself into the dust. In a diving sense, to turn around before my breaking point means I can get back to the cave entrance, and safety, without too much drama. And if drama did happen, I'd be fresh enough to handle whatever problems were thrown my way. Likewise, some novelists have talked about a similar process that has prevented them from suffering the curse of writer's block. When working at the page, they often turn in for the day while creatively *mid-flow*. This serves two important purposes. The first: a literary jumping-off point has been left for them, so the author need only to sit at their desk the next day and look at the last line to know exactly where they are taking the narrative. The second: emotionally, they are sure to arrive at work feeling refreshed, and not having not previously squeezed their creative juices to the maximum; they have energy and enthusiasm for the work ahead.

THE POWER OF PROCESS

Decompression shouldn't just happen when we're feeling physically or mentally fatigued. I have found it's equally important to take some personal time following a failed dive, or a disappointing event. I first accepted this idea in 2005 when Rick and I explored Cogol dei Veci in northern Italy. At the time, only one person had gone further than 2.5 kilometres (1.5 miles) into the cave, which is a long way in when moving underwater. However, we had set ourselves the challenging task of not only passing that milestone, but also of exploring the caves beyond. The trip would require us to camp inside, overnight, on a damp sand bank. Frustratingly, when we swam into sump two on a relay dive to explore and survey the cave while laying a series of guidelines, after a few hundred metres I lost my way. This happened partly through my inexperience, and I found myself unable to go any further. Rick was left to finish the job, and while the exploration was a success as a whole – we added over 1,000 metres (1,100 yards) of explored distance to the cave – I felt despondent. I couldn't shake the idea that I had let myself down and, as a consequence, held Rick back. On the journey home, I remember standing at the back of the ferry and quietly giving myself a talking to.

'Get back on it,' I thought. 'You need to dive as soon as you can to prove to yourself you can still do this . . .'

Given half the chance, I'd have gone back the very next day.

In reality, what I needed was some time to rest and reset. It is all too easy to overstretch our resources through fear, stress or disappointment. My desire to push myself again so soon was fuelled by the false idea that I had been a failure. But that urgency was propelled by ego and had I been able to return the next day, I probably would have performed no differently – I was knackered after all; I wouldn't have explored to the best of my ability. (Some kids do something similar during their exams after having become fearful of flunking, or when feeling the pressure from their parents. They study and revise until they are mentally exhausted and so aren't as sharp as they should be when the big day arrives. It is sometimes better to decompress for twenty-four hours beforehand.) Eventually, after recognising that I had become tired, and that there would be every chance to return to Italy at some point, I was able to let it go. But only once I had suitably recharged.

'Just take a bit of time,' I told myself. 'Relax about it. Learn some lessons and come back stronger.'

I did just that. Feeling rested and fully recovered, I later ventured into the Font Belle in southern France, which was a smaller and more complex cave than the Cogol dei Veci, but one I knew to be every bit as committing. I thrived. On reaching the limits of what had been explored previously, I pushed on, more relaxed and able to read the environment comfortably. I happily swam into the unknown without a thought for my disappointing performance in Italy.

What we do in our moments of decompression can be very important, especially while trying to process some of the more emotionally challenging events that have taken place. Exploring underwater caves, as I've already explained, can be a very intense business. There have been times where I have sensed the worst is about to happen and I was in no doubt that my time was up. While I accept that, without care, death underwater is a distinct possibility, I'd like to avoid it for as long as I can if possible – drowning in grisly circumstances within a flooded cave is pretty much guaranteed to spoil anyone's day. Strangely though, given my attitude to death, I have not been one to overthink or become stressed when mortal danger has presented itself. Instead, I tend to rationalise the situation, such as when I have lost my way, and avoid the urge to panic. Freaking out underwater is a self-fulfilling prophecy: a diver losing emotional control reduces their capacity to solve a problem in tight circumstances. It is only once I'm away from the cave safely that I will allow myself to reflect upon what has happened.

I have also experienced some unpleasant things while working on body recovery operations. As you can imagine, this can occasionally make for gruesome work, but I have always made a point of looking into the eyes of the person I'm trying to bring to the surface. I do this out of respect – to my mind I am partly engaging in an intimate conversation with the deceased, but it's also a slightly unusual way of checking in with my psyche. By looking death squarely in the face, I am asking myself a question: *Am I being emotionally upended by this situation?* I want to know if I'm experiencing an event a situation that might upset me again at some point in the future. And if that's the case, it is something I can make a point of dealing with once I am in a period of emotional decompression.

Thankfully, I have not yet been psychologically wounded in such a way that my world has come crashing down afterwards. Following on from a near-death experience, my response has usually been one of gratitude. *Thankfully, I'm still here to tell the tale.* And I have not seen anything so unsettling that I've been struck by the night terrors, felt the onset of PTSD or some other emotional injury. Instead, my only traumas have emerged from missed opportunities and unfulfilled expectations. The thought of leaving those deceased Finnish divers in the Plura cave system in Norway affected me for quite a while afterwards, though my upset was mainly a result of performance, and of not being able to bring closure to their families.

Any other emotional changes that I have experienced recently are a result of age. I have spoken to friends that have experienced a hard time after seeing or experiencing some unpleasantness underwater. Following on from our chats, I have been left to ponder the question: 'Is there something I should be worried about too? Or are my moods and grumpiness just a sign of getting a little bit older?' Thankfully, during moments of emotional decompression, I have taken the time to peek into the shadowy corners of my mind and come to the conclusion that it's very much the latter. In fact I have macabrely thought through the emotions of recovering Rick's body from a watery tomb and decided I'd be comfortable with the work, if the need ever arose.

I told him so once. I don't recall him being particularly delighted at the news. I think he plans to live forever.

REST AND DECOMPRESS: THE CHECKLIST

- Take time out. Draw fresh inspiration.
- Recognise fatigue. Rest if necessary.
- Process the past. Translate negative emotions into positive lessons.

LESSON #5

ONE BREATH AT A TIME

It's easy to feel panicked underwater. Passages can narrow into claustro-phobic dead ends. Equipment can fail at the worst possible moment. And a faulty rebreather, or a broken scooter can leave a cave diver making a headlong dash for the nearest airspace as their oxygen supply dwindles. It is essential to remain calm under pressure. Easier said than done, I know, but by utilising one simple technique it is possible to dissect a huge prob-lem into something more manageable, just by working towards three dis-tinct timescales – three seconds, three minutes, and three hours . . .

DAY SEVEN (PART ONE)
MONDAY 2 JULY 2018

We could have turned around. *Really, we should have turned around.* Four hours into the dive, it was clear to both Rick and myself that we were approaching the limits of how far we were able to go given the air remaining in our cylinders. When I checked the gauge, my first third of air was close to expiring. There was no question that we had to consider readying ourselves for the long push back, yet still we swam on through sumps five, six and seven, around 2 kilometres (1.2 miles) into Tham Luang, laying guidelines, all the while looking out for bodies in the water or some sign of life among the rocky banks. With hindsight, pushing ourselves to an acceptable edge was the right thing to do. In the moment, though, I felt edgy.

Ominous shadows seemed to drift and bob in the water around me, many of them human-shaped. At one point, in what I thought was the lowest part of the cave, I caught sight of some teenager-sized forms above me. My heart sank. *Was it some of the kids?* But having moved closer, I was able to pick out the curved edges of a body board, and then another. I counted four or five. They must have been used by a group of cavers who hadn't been able to swim across the lake that gathered here during dry season. When water had filled this particular section of Tham Luang, the polystyrene boards must have risen with it and they were now pinned to the roof in an eerie reminder of the storms raging outside.

At times, it was difficult to know which way to go, or how to navigate the underwater terrain. We were in unfamiliar territory, without a line to follow. As the ceiling rose in one section of the cave, a rock shelf angled up from the muddy floor and we had to crawl through what were shallows ahead. I used the water to buoy the equipment hanging about my body. After about 10 metres (thirty feet), I belly-flopped like a seal into the deeper pools and swam on. Later, in the pitch darkness, I wafted a hand and watched for how the sediment reacted around us. We were supposed to be working our way upstream into the hill. Determining downstream by checking the drifting particles, we'd then swim in the opposite direction into the main flow and hopefully towards a deeper chamber inside Tham Luang.

We pushed into a swirl chamber. This was unknown territory; neither of us had been this deep into Tham Luang before, and our plan that day had been to look for Pattaya Beach, an area located somewhere around the eighth chamber in the cave system and a spot where the authorities believed the boys might have found shelter.

I had around 30 metres (100 feet) of thick climbing rope still to spool out. The Thai Navy SEALs had been using it as a guideline and it was stuffed into a fertiliser bag. I'd also been carrying another 200 metres (650 feet) of polypropylene line to fix, the type usually used for UK explorations, and knowing that Rick wasn't going to suggest that we head back first (because he rarely did), I had planned on returning to the entrance after laying all of my line. At that point we would have no choice: to continue without a guideline was unthinkable. Mentally, there was a scheme in place and while we weren't breaking any self-established rules, we were definitely bending them. Rick and I had both passed the point of being able to exit the cave alone in the event of a mishap. We were dependent on one another, and the strong supporting currents on the way back to make a speedy exit before our air supply expired. The clock was ticking.

I focused on physiological control. During moments of last resort, I knew that one method of extending the air supply when moving underwater was 'skip breathing', in which a diver short on air pauses at the end of every inhalation, in effect taking one breath in the time usually used for two. Theoretically, this technique can help extend the air supply, and by a considerable amount, too. Meanwhile, if the same individual can visualise a more relaxed situation – at home, on a beach, or in the garden – it is also possible for them to slow their heart rate. I paused for a few seconds at the top and bottom of every breath. And swimming on into the blackness we followed an ascending cave roof into a new space, passing what turned out to be a 350-metre- (380-yard-) long passage, the largest flooded section of Tham Luang.

There was a very good reason for navigating a search dive by looking up and directly ahead rather than simply following the floor: we didn't want to miss any air pockets. Cave explorers are notorious for looking down, rather than up. In what has now become a famous search and rescue story, a cave diver in France once ran out of air and swam into a 'kicking water air bell', a dome-shaped air pocket above a vast, water-filled cavern. To alert any rescuers below, he smartly lowered his mask down to the cave floor on a line, the idea being that it might cause anyone swimming by to glance up. Happily, Frank Vasseur, the diver sent to look for him, understood the message. Upon discovering the mask, he followed the line to find a shaken, cold, but very relieved diver, who would almost certainly have perished had he relied on the search party to glance up at the right moment. While it was unlikely the Wild Boars had been stuck in a similar predicament, we weren't taking any chances.

Still, my apprehension was rising palpably with each passing breath; every inhalation and exhalation seemed to move in lockstep with an inner monologue.

'We should turn round soon,' I thought. *'We really need to turn round soon . . .'*

This urge was offset by a strong resolve to continue; it might have even been intuition, and I hadn't yet uttered those famous last words – *it'll be alright.* Though I sensed it wouldn't be long before they came. Luckily, I had a tactic for processing moments of high stress and I had previously planned my way out of potentially sticky situations by 'time-slicing' – a process in which I broke down the key moments ahead into three manageable chunks. Three seconds. Three minutes. Three hours. In other words, I looked to solve my problems in the short, medium and long term. As I peered up through the murky water to the ceiling above, my timeline was becoming clearly defined . . .

Three seconds: *Where's my next breath coming from?* When diving, I played a game in which, from time to time, I tapped at the spare regulator that dangled around my throat like a necklace. Just feeling it in its rightful place reassured me I'd be in great shape should the regulator in my mouth fail and I was left choking on water, which was always a stressful experience, especially if handled poorly. Reminding myself of where my spare was located helped to calm any short-term anxiety.

Three minutes: *How are we going to find the way forward?* The water around us was heavy with silt and visibility was poor. Staying near the ceiling gave me a visual route marker, but the overhanging rocks made for tricky work when pushing forwards and I had to weave between them by changing course and depth. I was also struggling to secure the line. It dangled in my hands as I swam. To fix it in position I would have to swim to the floor, either following a suitable stalagmite downwards or finding my way blindly in the dark waters below. As I worked, Rick hung back to check that I had effectively belayed the line, all the while keeping an eye out for anything that might have been taking place at my rear.

Three hours: *How are we going to get back safely?* While worrying, this issue was a little way back in my list of priorities – being unable to breathe, or getting lost in the dark were my most pressing concerns. Having said that, I still had to plan for our return. If something were to go wrong, the natural, human response would be to swim for the entrance as quickly as possible to reach safety, or help.

But bolting to the surface, which was over a kilometre (more than half a mile) away in this case, is often the worst thing a diver can do. It creates a sense of panic, and the more a diver panics, the quicker they breath; the quicker they breathe, the faster their air supply is used up, increasing the likelihood that an irreversible mistake will be made. There is also the reality that ascending too quickly might cause a nasty case of the bends.

But if that same diver can work their way through the first three stressful seconds to resolve their most pressing issue, then there is every chance their medium- and long-term problems will be solvable too. In my case, I had to think about breathing first and navigating second. Over a number of years I had also made friends with the sense of fear that could surge through me during a dive, and so I reminded myself of similar situations in which I had successfully negotiated an issue in the past and survived. *I would be OK.* And I was right to remain calm. The passage roof was opening up ahead of us and I could tell there was an air pocket above. We had made our way into the ninth chamber.

Then everything changed in an instant. Rick was sniffing the air; I was too. *Was that the smell of rotting flesh?* I sensed movement in my peripheral vision. There was a noise. And when I turned, our ideas and plans were tipped upside down. *The Wild Boars were alive.* I saw all thirteen of them standing on the bank. And suddenly a new set of problems had been presented to me. My mind raced.

Three seconds: *Take one breath at a time.*

Three minutes: *Were the boys OK?*

Three hours: *Could we make it out in one piece?*

THE POWER OF TIME-SLICING

It is so easy to let circumstances run away with us in a moment of high stress, such as the one we faced that day in Tham Luang. Over thousands of years, human nature and the evolutionary process have primed us to react quickly when danger emerges. Sadly, while that might have kept us alive when trying to outrun a sabre-toothed tiger, our nervous system has since become notorious for making some spectacularly poor choices under pressure. Rather than rationally analysing the situation we're in and making a more considered decision, we sometimes buckle under emotional strain and react inappropriately. One time, during a torrential thunderstorm, my car aquaplaned and rolled on a motorway. The vehicle flipped and skidded, and flipped

again, eventually coming to a to halt on its wheels in the middle
of the busy fast lane. I checked to see if the passenger alongside
me was hurt in any way. She shook her head.

'OK, I'm fine too. That's good . . .'

In an instant, everything changed. I began working through
my mental checklist.

Am I badly hurt? No. Good.

Is anyone else badly hurt? No. Also good.

How were we going to check on the passenger in the back seat?

Where are my glasses?

How the hell am I going to get us off this motorway?

But while my friend was physically in good shape, emotionally
she was melting down. Without warning, I heard the passenger
door open and watched, helplessly, as she staggered around the
car towards the back door, oblivious to the fact we had come to
rest in the fast lane of the motorway. She had completely forgotten
the first rule of any emergency situation: look after yourself first
or join the casualty list.

Time-slicing is an invaluable tool in such a crisis. This concept
had been drilled into me through twenty years working in
computer network engineering, because when a computer runs
too many applications at once, it can slow down, or drop some of
the tasks it might have been working through. Humans, like
computers, also tend to overheat and perform inefficiently when
overloaded with stress, or when dealing with too many tasks.
Having a traumatic car accident on a motorway, for example,
would be enough to send anyone's internal hard drive into chaos.
The key to dealing with these moments of overload is to scale the
bigger problem down into a series of manageable tasks over set
periods of time.

Three seconds: *Am I badly injured? Where am I? Is the situation going to get worse? Take one breath at a time . . .*

Three minutes: *Does anyone else need urgent attention? Can we move? How do we negotiate the traffic so we can get to the side of the road?*

Three hours: *How are we going to get assistance? And what the hell are we going to do for a ride home?*

But the importance of time-slicing really struck home during an exploration in 2002, in the early phases of my cave-diving career. At that time I enjoyed visiting the Lot, a region in southern France that was regarded as a holidaymakers' dream in the summer, with almost guaranteed sunshine, fresh-water beaches and scenery. Underground, however, the region was just as appealing. The limestone landscape, with its exceptionally long and deep waterways, had formed an ideal spot for experienced cavers and cave divers worldwide. When I arrived, I had a challenge in mind: this would be the first time I had ever used a rebreather in such a large network of tunnels and I was hoping to visit the end of a number of renowned caves in the region. I would also be working alone.

The first couple of dives went well and I felt ready to tackle my first major objective, which was to pass the second sump in the Fontaine Saint Georges, an area located beneath the village of Montvalent. This exploration would involve an underwater journey of nearly two kilometres (just over a mile), where I would reach depths of nearly 80 metres (260 feet), at which point I'd follow the cave to the surface in a series of slow, controlled steps so I could decompress. I would then have to repeat the whole process in reverse on the way back, decompressing out of the cave and towards safety. There was little doubt that my limited experience would be tested while operating at such depths. Timing my journey to the surface would prove challenging too.

Cave divers usually carry large numbers of air cylinders and this dive was no exception. As well as my back-mounted rebreather, I was also hauling five tanks, which had been secured to either side of my body. Swimming with that amount of equipment was slow, so to speed my progress I was using a scooter, and my dive plan was to advance to the top of a gravel slope around 1 kilometre (0.6 miles) into the cave. Once there, I would jettison some of the cylinders for a break-glass-in-case-of-emergency decompression on the way back, if I needed to. I would then continue onwards, down the slope, into the lowest depths of Saint Georges, before emerging into a dry passage on the other side. Like a mountaineer having reached the summit, I would then have to reverse the entire process before returning to civilisation in time for a well-earned can of Diet Coke and a custard cream biscuit.

To a lot of people, the very idea of dealing with such a large number of tasks alone in an unfamiliar and underwater environment might have sounded rash, but as far as I was concerned, cave diving was a sport that twinned problem solving with consequences. This was a combination that appealed to me because it sharpened the mind, and created a situation where I was responsible for any choices I might make. For example, if I wanted to build and try out a piece of equipment or test a new procedure, the responsibility was on me and only me. That made the experience all the more real. That's not to say I am an adrenaline junkie – I've long stressed that if ever a diver felt their heart racing, they were doing something very wrong. Instead, I enjoyed committing to a task where any moments of failure carried serious implications. By pushing my personal limits with a rebreather, alone in Fontaine Saint Georges, that philosophy was very much being put into practice. It was bound to be an interesting experience.

At first, the dive seemed to be going well. My equipment was behaving and I reached the 1-kilometre (0.6-mile) mark quite comfortably, where I dropped off my emergency cylinders as planned. I then spent a couple of minutes mentally preparing for the tasks to come – and there was little margin for error. Operating at a depth of 70metres (230 feet), alone in the pitch-black, close to 1.5 kilometres (nearly a mile) into a flooded cave, required composure. I was definitely out of my comfort zone, but once readied, I pointed my scooter down the slope, pressed the 'on' switch and shot off, following the guideline into the inky abyss.

Everything happens very fast when scootering downhill in an underwater cave. For starters, it's important to follow the guideline – losing sight of the rope or tangling myself up in it would have ruined the dive, if not the whole day. I also had to monitor my rebreather, adjusting the oxygen content of the gas I was inhaling, while adding more gas to ensure there was enough volume to actually draw breath. This would prove a delicate balancing act. Controlling my buoyancy was equally important, and this was done by either adding or venting air from both my drysuit and the secondary wing attached to my back. If all of this sounds complicated, that's because it was. At various moments, the experience felt not too dissimilar to patting my head and rubbing my tummy at exactly the same time.

Getting any one of these tasks wrong had the potential to snowball into chaos: there was every chance my body would become pinned to the passage ceiling, or dumped in a messy landing at the bottom of the slope, where I would find myself lost in a blinding silt cloud, with no idea where the exit was. Most pressingly, I'd likely have a rebreather full of water, so drawing in air would be impossible. As I descended, slowly and cautiously, watching as the numbers on my dive computer ticked up, every increment indicated my increasing depth and a growing commitment to the job. There was no turning back now. I felt the water chill around me.

Handily, I had managed to maintain a fair semblance of control, but having reached the bottom of the cave and levelled out, my exploration took a tricky turn. *My guideline had finished!* I desperately looked around for another line as I whizzed along on the scooter, until I realised it had been severed by previous floods and was now wafting somewhere in the water. Instinctively, I tied on my spare line reel to the frayed end, knowing it would at least help me to relocate a rough path back to the entrance should I need it, but I could feel the panic rising and I worked to push it back down. My head jerked this way and that as I searched the ceiling for some clue as to the whereabouts of a vertical tunnel I knew would take me to the other side of the second sump.

It didn't take me long to realise I had missed the way on. Caves such as Fontaine Saint Georges have a high water flow, in which the rapid currents scour away deposits of really fine silt from the surrounding rock. I could see banks of the stuff everywhere and no sign of my escape route. Worse still, even the slightest waft of my dive fins, or a murmur of bubbles from the rebreather, was enough to unsettle the sediment in the water. Muddy clouds smoked about me, reducing the visibility to zero and slowing my progress. But I couldn't waste any more time at this depth because I didn't have the spare cylinders for even more hours of additional decompression, or the capacity in my rebreather. Feeling my heart rate spiking, I retraced my journey and instantly realised my mistake. *I had moved out of the main flow of the cave!* Knowing the way on must be in the roof somewhere, I ascended into what I convinced myself was the correct vertical passage, up in the farthest reaches of the tunnel.

Trouble struck me almost immediately. The passage I had moved into was narrow, barely chest-width, and the visibility had dropped to close to zero. Still, I forced myself upwards, but I had become a human scouring pad in a drainpipe, scraping silt from the walls, which darkened the world around me even more. As the passage started to squeeze me in a claustrophobic bear hug, I was fast becoming entombed. I cursed myself. *Overfocused, inexperienced, task loaded, idiot*! I had gone too far, too quickly. But there was no time to listen to my inner critic. Deciding that one good heave upwards should have seen me into a larger passage above, I pushed. And pushed.

The single rebreather I had been using that day came affixed with two small bags called counter lungs that were attached to my chest. Two electronic controllers were positioned alongside them and they worked to keep me alive: in effect these 'computers' ensured the correct oxygen levels were being maintained in my breathing gas. This arrangement allowed the machine to store and process my exhaled breath, and it was a fairly effective set-up with one major drawback: when the counter lungs were restricted it became impossible for the wearer to breathe out. That carried the potential to create a very precarious situation, especially if a diver became jammed between two surfaces.

I was now in that very precarious situation.

Rather than popping out into a larger passage, my committed

heave had jammed me into an even tighter section of the rift. I had been blinded by sediment in the water and the rock walls pinched at my body so tightly that I was unable to breathe. I couldn't move my arms, I could barely wriggle my legs, and my chest was constricted. When I then glanced down, I realised in horror that both the displays on my rebreather's electronic controllers were dead. *Had they been damaged?* The severity of the situation was like a bomb going off in my head. *I'm a mile inside a completely flooded and pitch-black cave. My rebreather's failing and my oxygen supply is about to die. I'm pinned tight, with no real idea where the exit might be and stuck at an extreme depth.*

Even if I was able to resolve each problem individually, which seemed unlikely, I had no idea what level of oxygen was contained in the gas I had been breathing. That meant it was impossible to calculate accurately the amount of time needed to decompress before surfacing. In a brief moment of panic, I imagined a nightmarish case of the bends and the hospital wheelchair[*] that would await me after many hours of failed and very painful medical treatment. For a moment, my situation seemed hopeless; too many things had gone wrong and recovering from them all felt impossible. I would never again experience the warm sunshine and campsite chat that I'd enjoyed in Lot earlier that morning.

Somehow, though, I was able to course correct emotionally. Sure, the puzzle I'd found myself in seemed incomprehensible, like the opening moves in a high-stakes chess match with far too

---

[*] Decompression sickness or the bends is divided into two categories: type one is loosely classified as 'simple', or pain only. Type two is more serious and can cause an injury to the central nervous system. In severe cases, damage to the spinal cord can leave a diver with permanently limited mobility and loss of sensation.

many variables. But if I could prioritise the tasks ahead, dealing with them in the shortest timeframe I could imagine, then maybe I could extricate myself from my jam relatively safely. The first step was to pick a task.

'Easy,' I thought. 'Work out how to breathe, it'll only take three seconds.'

Easing my way down, I found just enough space between my chest and the two rock walls to allow my counter lungs to inflate. The rush of what I hoped was breathable air into my lungs felt like a massive relief.

My second task was then to spend a few seconds figuring out exactly *what* I was breathing. Examining the electronic controllers, I realised that rather than being broken, my thrashing around in the rift had caused the switches to turn off. *They were still working!* I quickly set about restarting the system; a process I knew had to be performed very carefully at such a depth, as it could prove fatal. (Choosing the wrong option on the menu might have flooded the rebreather with oxygen, which would have triggered convulsions and a very unpleasant death.) *But what other choice did I have?* Working through the problem helped me to refocus psychologically. My heart rate was slowing; my breathing felt controlled, and I was able to progress towards a medium-term goal. *Perhaps if I allowed myself to plan three minutes ahead, I'd be able to wriggle down from the rift, locate the guideline and make my way to the exit? At which point I'd figure out my decompression schedule and avoid that bloody wheelchair.*

I had visualised a path to success; the solutions to each problem had arrived one-by-one and with every task completion I moved slowly, *surely*, towards safety. By the time I had moved down the rift and reached the bottom of the gravel slope once more, my terror had changed to quiet resolve. I knew the decompression schedule on my dive computer would be wrong – the rebreather had been switched off, so the gas I had been breathing wouldn't match what the dive computer had expected. My problem was that I didn't know just how wrong it was. After some convoluted mental arithmetic, I added what I considered to be an appropriate amount of time to my decompression schedule and made my journey back towards the entrance of Fontaine Saint Georges.

As I mentioned in the last chapter, decompression is a meditative process for me. While waiting for the minutes to tick by, I reflected on the events of the past hour, and how I had underestimated the challenge. I realised that laying the guideline for myself and finding the way through the cave alone was much harder than following a path set by another diver. Most importantly, it delivered a severe lesson in just how quickly things could go wrong underwater – and how hard it could be to recover from them. But somehow, *I had*.

Having eventually emerged from decompression unscathed, I decided that from that moment on I would face complex situations in three timeframes: organising problems into three seconds, three minutes and then longer, perhaps three hours or even days. I wouldn't move on to the second set of problems without having sorted out the first. I would split my mental capacity into time slices in advance, much like a computer would. Then, in moments of stress, such as those regarding safety or breathing, I would focus entirely on the urgent priorities, discarding any lower priority tasks if the situation became overwhelming. That way I would increase my chances of surviving unharmed.

I later discovered that this practice could be applied to all manner of stressful events, one of which was the buying of my last house. Whenever I had been in a full-time job in the past, securing a mortgage had seemed relatively easy. In order to find out how much I could borrow against my salary, I only had to hand over a few months' worth of payslips to the broker. But all that changed once I became self-employed. The process was transformed into a contractual wrestling match with all manner of red tape and legalese, and I can remember the sinking feeling of being presented with an inch-thick bundle of paperwork by the postman one morning. Inside were all sorts of forms and contracts that required me to dig up various sets of accounts or documentation, or to perform some display of mathematical gymnastics. The workload ahead was so daunting that it became a struggle to avoid giving up.

'This won't happen,' I thought, despondently. 'I just can't do it.'

Then I remembered my situation in Fontaine Saint Georges. I broke down what felt like an overwhelming and insurmountable problem into a list of tasks in order of priority and worked out whether they needed to be completed in the short, medium or long term.

Three seconds: *One breath at a time . . . Read the first form.*

Three minutes: *OK, now scan through the documents and get a rough idea of what paperwork you'll need in order to apply for this mortgage.*

Three hours: *Call the accountant, get your tax returns from the past few years and do the sums.*

Slowly the forms were filled in. And I bought the house.

The technique really can be applied to just about any nerve-wracking event. Say you are due to give a presentation to your peers, a situation that always causes your palms to sweat and your nights to become restless. It might help to time-slice the situation down into short-, medium- and long-term stages.

Three seconds: *One breath at a time. Relax and remember to speak slowly.*

Three minutes: *Remember the message you're trying to communicate. Use your slides and charts effectively.*

Three hours: *Follow up with the group. Was everything clear? Is there any other documentation to hand out?*

By following this procedure, it's possible to avoid a psychological overload, even during the most challenging of circumstances.

Above all, it's important to remember just one thing: *breathe.*

ONE BREATH AT A TIME: THE CHECKLIST

- Prioritise critical tasks. Start with a breath. (Three seconds.)
- Consider your situation. Make a plan. (Three minutes.)
- Progress towards your goal. Look long term. (Three hours.)

LESSON #6

EXPECT THE UNEXPECTED

To understand how best to expect the unexpected, it helps to acknowledge the unpredictability of pretty much everything that happens in life. Our day-to-day existence rarely goes exactly as planned, and occasionally we'll be blindsided by overwhelming events that hit us from left field. Pandemics happen. Earthquakes wobble cities. Lightning bolts strike. Or, as John Lennon once sang in the 1981 track 'Beautiful Boy (Darling Boy)': 'Life's what happens to you while you're busy making plans.' Shocking events aren't always entirely unforeseen; it's just the timing that feels unsettling and the fact that it's happening to us. However, by learning one or two thought processes we can quickly accept the unexpected and cope more effectively.

DAY SEVEN (PART TWO)
MONDAY 2 JULY 2018

We had been wrong: *the kids were alive*. It was time to rethink our plans.

I heard Rick counting out the children.

'How many are you?' I shouted.

A voice at the back of the group yelled back.

Thirteen.

I couldn't believe what I was seeing and hearing. There hadn't been any fatalities so far and at least one of the Wild Boars understood a smattering of English. From the gloom, another kid asked if they would be going home that day.

'No, not today,' said Rick.

I chimed in. 'There's two of us. You have to dive. We are coming. It's OK. Many people are coming. Many, many people and we are the first. Many people come . . .'

But as I waded forward to greet them, I was struck by a chilling thought. Before our first dive during the search for Eric Establie in the Ardèche Gorge, Rick and I had agreed to treat the stranded diver as a threat. This might sound strange, and certainly, none of the background information that had been shared with us suggested in any way that he was a dangerous or unstable individual, but people act in dangerous and unstable ways when they have been trapped underground for days. There was the slimmest chance that Eric might have seen us emerging from the water and lashed out in a crazed state of mind. Or he could have made a grab for one of our rebreathers, damaging a vital piece of equipment in the process and stranding all of us inside.

Given we were now in the ninth chamber, the furthest anyone from the rescue team had so far travelled into Tham Luang, it felt sensible to follow protocols that were similar to those we had first established in the Ardèche Gorge. This seemed particularly appropriate given the people we were rescuing. Kids could be unpredictable; the Wild Boars were probably in a state of high anxiety. It would only take one excitable grab at a cylinder, mask or regulator for one of us to be marooned.

'Rick, we need to de-kit on the opposite side of the passage,' I said.

He nodded, and once stripped of our technical gear we waded towards the bank.

I am a firm believer in visualising negative situations to prepare myself emotionally. For days I had gone to bed imagining the horrific scene that might have greeted me underwater were I to swim into a cavern filled with bobbing corpses. I was just as prepared for an event where we stumbled into a group of survivors still living among the dead. There might have been a moment where Rick and I were faced with the ghastly business of separating the breathing from the deceased, and some of them might have been in various stages of decomposition. While this was an undeniably macabre state of mind to place myself in, it meant I would be able to cope when a crisis struck.

Now all thirteen boys were alive, I had to ditch the negative defence mechanisms immediately and then plan for the new reality. *Somehow we had to get these kids out.* There was a whole list of tasks needing to be completed, many of which, if I was brutally honest, I hadn't considered in days because the chances of the

Wild Boars being alive had seemed so slim. To set the ball rolling, I urged the boys back onto the slope. I wanted to anchor the guideline I would be swimming with as far up the bank as possible in case the waters rose even higher. That way, we could easily locate their position in what looked like a very narrow space. I pinned the polypropylene line into the ground using the handle of my reel as a makeshift tent peg.

Sometimes in crisis events of this kind, it only takes one incident to break the tension. There was a loud splash behind me, and when I turned to look, I saw that Rick had tumbled back while making his way up the slippery incline. A couple of misplaced steps had caused him to fall awkwardly into the water and the kids were suddenly laughing and pointing, though having spotted his gaffe, God knows what must have been going through their minds. I'm sure one or two must have doubted the chances of two middle-aged men getting them out in one piece, especially as one of them was wearing a rubber ring on his back for buoyancy. Rick staggered to his feet, and as we scaled the bank and investigated the tunnels that had been the kids' home for ten days, they began interrogating us in broken English.

What day is it?
We are hungry . . .
Where are you from?
'I am very happy,' said one of the boys at being found.

'We are very happy too,' I responded, capturing everything on a video camera that had been given to us by the Thai Navy SEALs earlier in the dive. It had been passed over to me as we submerged into the water beyond chamber three. The military had wanted us to film the line configuration at the Sam Yaek junction, hoping it might provide a visual guide for their subsequent dives. That one piece of equipment had now become a life-saving device: it would document that all thirteen of the boys were alive while giving us a reference for the state of the cave and what could, and could not, be done for them while they remained trapped inside.

'Don't lose that,' said Rick pointing to the digital recorder. 'It's now the most valuable camera in the world.'

I nodded, but I remained concerned. *How the hell were we going to leave these kids in a relatively healthy state of mind?* They were clearly tired, hungry and scared. The conditions they had been living in were squalid. The cave was 20 metres (65 feet) high, dark and chilly. The ledge was narrow and sloped steeply upwards at 45 degrees. The muddy floor was damp and slippery. Further up the slope the boys had hacked out a makeshift ledge in the mud, which gave them somewhere to perch on what was a steep incline that led down to the water. I would later learn that the boys hadn't eaten for over a week, and to stay alive they were drinking filthy water from the rising flood. Hygienically, the Wild Boars were struggling, and the bank smelled like a public toilet. (Though given they hadn't eaten for days, that was not as problematic as it could have been.) It would also later be reported that their time spent in the cave had been unsurprisingly emotional: on some days, Coach Ek led a series of meditations to lift the spirits. On others, the boys would break down and weep. Many of them, I imagined, were wrongly assuming that the worst was now over, and they would soon be reunited with their worried families. The reality for them was that the worst was yet to come. Positivity was vital for their emotional stability, so I turned to some of the techniques I had used when working with the kids from my Cub Scout pack in Bristol.

'They're a bit older,' I thought. 'And they're not as small as the Cubs at home, but I'll just have to pretend.'

One technique I thought might work was a shouted version of *The Grand Howl* – a morale-boosting chant in which everybody was asked to stand in a circle at the beginning and end of every Cubs session, and urged to do their best. The pack then responded with a shout.

We will do our best!

I sensed that getting the Wild Boars into a similar headspace would help to create a positive mood. But if I also filmed the kids while they were singing, it might also serve as a morale booster for the people working and waiting outside – the demoralised engineers, the distressed families, the Thai Navy SEALs and some of the other workers who had been labouring tirelessly. Just three hours earlier, I had been in that same dispirited frame of mind. Now the unexpected had happened and I was course correcting as quickly as possible. And so I gathered the kids together and pointed my camera their way, asking them to cheer for each of the groups I knew were waiting at dive base, which had been established in chamber three – the Americans, the Canadians, the Australians, the Thais – before doing everything I could to encourage the Wild Boars by explaining that everyone outside would soon be planning their eventual rescue.

Really, it was all I could do. Other than reassuring them that we would swim to the surface to tell the others of their survival, I was utterly powerless. Somewhat boldly, I then promised the children I would return with supplies, but as we made our way to the other bank to collect our equipment, Rick made it clear he thought that I had overreached a little. The truth is, I had really meant it. I felt absolutely responsible for those twelve kids and their coach who, without realising it, were perched on a knife-edge between survival and death. With a heavy sense of foreboding, I finned away down the dark tunnel.

The journey back was heavy work. I crawled across the rocky ridge of chamber seven, though beyond that I was able to swim fairly smoothly for much of the way thanks to a strong current that propelled me from the rear. My anxiety was then amplified by a nasty, shoulder-width tunnel just beyond the sixth chamber that took some effort to squeeze through. While wearing two side-mounted cylinders, it required every ounce of effort to force myself beyond the squeeze, and the white-knuckle tension that accompanied every push was only heightened by the water flowing inside. The tunnel was half full. That meant that anyone passing through was exposed to the disorienting experience of trying to breath the air above the water, without being able to inhale comfortably because the rocky roof was too low.

But there was no other option. Given I was trying to preserve the fading air in my cylinders – in case should I need it later – I had to make the most of any air pockets. Having your face half submerged is one of the most intimidating situations when swimming through a tight squeeze in a flooded cave. The brain plays all sorts of tricks, mainly by triggering a reaction where the diver instinctively rises up to inhale, even though there is very little room to manoeuvre. Meanwhile, every wriggle or push causes the water to splash and surge, which can be very confusing – it becomes almost impossible to distinguish the water from the air pocket above. The fact that the diver's body is also being weighed down by all sorts of heavy diving equipment means that moving through such a squeeze can be terrifying and disorienting, even when there's a regulator to breathe from.

Experience helped me stay calm. With every passing metre, I became increasingly confident of making it back to the cave entrance untroubled by any air issues, though the section just before the fourth chamber had proven to be particularly problematic on the way in, and so it would on the way out. Inside it was dark, the water churned with sediment, and the guideline running through it had become slack due to repeated pulling – something an experienced cave diver would never normally do on a route of that kind*. Worse, it had been wound around a number of complex stalactites and other rock formations and it took a lot of effort to feel my way through carefully. If Rick or I were to find trouble at any point, given our limited air supplies, it would very quickly become a race against the clock.

By the time I made my way through and was approaching Tham Luang's third chamber, I could hear the engineers' pumps running as they churned away more and more of the water rushing into Tham Luang. *We were nearly home.* Given that Rick and I were the only people to know that the Wild Boars were still alive, and that I had the video evidence to prove it, remaining focused was the priority. Both of us were feeling a huge weight of responsibility, but there was really no point in bolting for the exit – picking up an injury on the way, or worse not making the surface at all, would have been a disaster for everyone involved. Instead, I moved slowly and steadily, ticking off the obstacles one at a time, keen to avoid any mistakes.

---

* The military divers had been using thick lines to withstand the currents. These were easy to pull on, but a large number of divers had been using them. This caused them to become slack. To ease our passage forward we used the lines ourselves, while being careful not to worsen their already poor state.

My head broke water. I instantly recognised the hustle and bustle of the dive base chamber three where one or two Navy SEALs were moving in the distance.

Waving, I shouted out. 'We've found the kids! They're still alive.'

One man sauntered over. He didn't seem to comprehend the enormity of what I was telling him.

'The kids are alive – '

'Are you OK?' he said, looking at me as if I was making an incredible fuss over nothing.

'I'm fine, but the children are alive.'

I pointed to the digital camera. *The children are alive!*

Finally, the penny seemed to drop. The SEAL, now understanding exactly what was happening, shifted into a higher gear. There was shouting. An excited hubbub kicked up around us; the sound of yelled instructions ricocheted around the cavern. Previously demoralised soldiers and engineers who had been slouched on rocks, or walking slowly between tasks, suddenly moved at an urgent speed. The previous indifference to our efforts was replaced by backslaps and handshakes; people wanted to talk to us; for the first time in the entire mission, somebody even reached out a hand and offered to carry my equipment.

I looked around for a figure of authority. I understood there were now protocols that needed to be respected, especially when it came to the custody of what was now vital evidence, and I was keen not to break them. The camera had to go to the most appropriate person in charge and in this case, that was the Thai Navy's Dive Supervisor, who was responsible for keeping an eye on all of the work that was taking place underwater, which theoretically included the activities of Rick and myself. I handed him the camera.

'The children,' I said once more, hoping he would understand.

Whether the camera was then passed on to an aide as we spoke, or if it was downloaded onto a laptop, I'm really not sure, because the cave was in chaos. What I do know is that the video somehow made its way out of Tham Luang and into the wider world long before Rick and I did. We went back to our pokey room and attempted to figure out the grand complexities of dragging those kids through 2.5 kilometres (1.5) of underground waterway – a cave that had rebuffed some of the most experienced rescue divers in the business. We also had to explain what was going on to a number of people who had been fairly resistant to our involvement in the first place. How that was likely to go down, I had no idea.

It was time to prepare for our debrief.

HOW TO ACCEPT THE UNEXPECTED

Many so-called 'unprecedented events' occur much more frequently than you would think. Since 1994, the UK National Lottery has created millionaires at a rate of over 220 a year. Meanwhile over half the United Kingdom's adult population haven't written a will and yet the one certainty in life is that we're all going to die. Weirdly, I have found that the difficulty most people have when dealing with a shock event is, firstly, that the shock event is happening to *them*. ('Why me?' they say.) And secondly, that it is happening *now*. ('What bad timing!') As humans, we are reluctant to accept the more unpleasant realities of life, so we block a great many of them from our minds; we figure that they are too uncomfortable to look at, or not worth considering yet, but that can leave us unable to cope when a lightning strike event actually occurs.

The one horrible 'surprise' we most commonly have to deal with is the death of a parent. I know it's upsetting to visualise, so maybe you should skip this paragraph if you're not emotionally prepared, but when a grieving son or daughter expresses their utter shock at one of their parents passing away, it always strikes me as being slightly strange. It is entirely expected that somebody who is twenty, thirty, or forty years older than their kids should pass away first. And by the way, I am not saying that anyone should not be grieving, or that their loss isn't overwhelmingly painful. Rather, I am pointing out that it is, sadly, predictable: it's the natural order of things, as the Disney movie, *The Lion King* clearly explains when it talks about the Circle of Life. (Having lost one parent already, I do understand the difficulties of death, but I have always felt that funerals should be a celebration of someone's life rather than the sad events they can often be. I have also found that it's helped me to begin the separation process in advance, and in private, by contemplating and accepting that we will outlive our parents. It's one way of softening the blow when it does arrive.)

In much the same way, I should have been ready for the possibility of the Wild Boars surviving, but I had forgotten my own rule: *the unexpected can be handled*. Instead I had wrongly assumed that any chance of their still being alive had vanished, especially as the days passed by and the waters rose. Having then taken my eye off the ball, I was caught briefly off guard when we'd found all of them, in fairly good shape, in the ninth chamber. The discovery was truly surprising.

What Rick and I did next was *to accept the situation*. I stored our kit away from the kids in case one of them then acted irresponsibly or aggressively. I performed a headcount and checked for any serious injuries. I reassured the group that everybody was doing their utmost to help them escape and that more people would be coming. I then attempted to lift their morale and that of everyone working outside by filming a series of waves and cheers from the kids. I didn't panic or allow myself to crumble. Rather, I ran through a checklist – a *Library of Plans* – of what I thought would be suitable in such a situation and then worked through it accordingly.

In many ways, I take a similar attitude when driving. Sure, I can't predict that an accident will happen ahead of me, or that one of my tyres might blow out while cruising in the fast lane of a motorway. What I can do, however, is to ready myself for all manner of surprising events. Don't get me wrong: I've never felt the need to load up the boot with tools, defibrillators and cutting equipment. But I do have a length of rope, a fire extinguisher, some blankets and jump leads, as well as a comprehensive first-aid kit. You'd be surprised at the times this armoury of resources has come in handy.

Last year, I was driving home one night after a particularly tough day at work. I was knackered, but as I pulled into my street I saw a couple of people standing in the middle of the road. They were helping somebody who was flat-out on the floor and every part of me wanted to drive around them and go home. I really didn't want to accept that something unexpected and potentially stressful was taking place. Then my sense of duty kicked in and I acknowledged the situation.

'I suppose I'd better stop and get the first-aid kit out . . .'

By the time I had pulled over to see exactly what was going on, it was clear that the person on the floor, although unconscious, was being cared for adequately. 'An ambulance is on its way,' said one of the helpers. Everything seemed to be under control. Then with a creeping sense of dread, I realised that everything *wasn't* OK. Nobody had thought to keep an eye on the passing traffic, and there was a good chance that somebody might get run over before the emergency services had even arrived. I helped out as best I could, guiding a series of cars past the scene until the victim had been placed on a stretcher and driven away.

Acceptance is even more important when cave diving. I am wary of divers who think they are invincible. Naively, they assume that bad luck won't come their way and when it does – which is an inevitable reality for any cave diver – they are entirely unprepared to cope, both practically and psychologically. Rather than taking this slapdash approach, I prefer to bring the concept of Murphy's Law into consideration ('Anything that can go wrong will go wrong'), especially when I'm tired. I put various checking systems in place, well in advance of an accident actually happening, so I can catch any potential moments of inattention. Then I work hard to remain flexible at all times. To borrow an old military adage, I prepare for the worst and hope for the best.

In any pursuit or activity that requires a high level of diligence, you can spot the people who might, eventually, succumb to a terrible accident. They are usually the ones who cut corners and take risks; they fail to cross the T's and dot their I's. A lot of the time, those characters are able to survive on flair alone and, for the most part, they get away with a *laissez-faire* attitude. Eventually though, when confronted with danger, they struggle, or worse, they die. In knife-edge situations, flair often proves to be an inadequate escape route.

But corner-cutting is a tricky to habit to quit (until it is fatal) because the very result of getting away with something hardens the motivation within a person to take those same risks again. (An enquiry into the Challenger space shuttle disaster in 1986 called this psychology 'the normalisation of deviance'.) People become emboldened to cheat; they believe they can skip the processes of due diligence because doing so has worked for them in the past, but the truth is this: a person will always believe they are able to get away with something, or cut corners until the very minute where it becomes impossible. And by then, it's usually too late to change course.

THE LIBRARY OF PLANS

Acceptance is only the first stage in dealing with an unexpected situation; the second requires a trip into what I call the Library of Plans. Usually, I like to visualise this as a dusty, old room stacked full of leather-bound books. Each one contains a plan, or an idea, for tackling a problematic situation I've thought through in the comfort of my own home. Often, both the problems and my solutions are based upon past experiences, advice from peers, educational programmes on TV, courses, lectures and books.

Sometimes, though, a plan emerges from musing on a 'What if . . .?' question. So, when the unexpected *does* happen, by going into the Library of Plans, it's possible to find something suitable without having to re-invent the wheel. In Tham Luang, I did exactly this, and faced with the twin challenge of children that were slightly older than my Cub group and the language barrier, I reached for a 'book' and found the idea of The Grand

Howl, before twisting it into a morale-boosting cheer. It worked too, using peer pressure and the group dynamic to lift the boys' mood.

Building a mental library of this kind requires some effort at first, but eventually, adding new books to the shelves can become almost second nature, and it can be done in two ways: the psychological and the practical. The psychological method requires us to play a hypothetical game, either alone or with a friend. Named, *What's the worst that can happen?*, it begins with a situation and an imagined problem, such as losing a passport, which is always a stressful predicament. The game then requires me to ask: 'What's the worst that can happen?' From there, the idea is to beat my opponent (or myself) with a list of resulting issues that are supposed to ascend in severity. If you are unable to get to a point in the game where a meteorite is crashing into Earth, or nuclear war has broken out, you'll need to think bigger!

For example:

I've lost my bus pass on the way home from the pub.

There's nobody about.

There are no streetlights. It's dark.

It's raining . . . And I forgot to bring a coat!

My phone is out of battery and it's about to die.

I'm miles away from civilisation.

It's Sunday, and the shops are shut.

I trip on the kerb and hit my head.

Lightning strikes!

An ambulance arrives, but crashes en route to the hospital.

The surgeon is on strike and my life-saving operation is delayed.

'We come to you with breaking news . . . A meteorite is on collision course for the Atlantic Ocean, where it's expected to wreak havoc on the planet.'

The latter part of this list is doom-laden fantasy, but it's helpful to look at the early disasters to see how they can be prevented. This game can also be applied in advance to some of the more difficult events we might have to endure in real life, such as the loss of a parent, the breakup of a relationship, or even the stressful first day spent working at a new job. By wargaming those situations in advance and then playing *What's the worst that can happen?*, we can plan for many different scenarios in safety and comfort. After all, it is much simpler to modify and execute an existing procedure than it is to develop an idea from scratch in the heat of the moment.

The second technique for expanding an internal book collection is much more practical – *simply write your ideas down.*

The very concept for the Library of Plans came about during a phase in which I had allowed the rescue aspect of my cave-diving career to eat into my life. I didn't make space for other things; I planned too much, and I was forever predicting what *might* happen while underwater, and to the nth degree. As a consequence, I built up and imagined a portfolio of solutions for all manner of problems. My overzealous planning soon crept into everything I did. It started to become overwhelming. Eventually, I decided the best way to manage the situation was to create some order with the Library of Plans, and then to write everything down, which was where my blue folder came into play.*

---

* Of the few photos of Rick and myself that appeared during the rescue, I was 1) usually frowning, and 2) carrying the blue folder. As I have mentioned earlier in the book, it provided a reference point as to how we should operate throughout..

Instead of mentally game planning for every problem that might happen during a rescue mission, I began to put together various lists, each one packed with procedures and requirements for core rescue scenarios. By doing so, I knew that if an issue did arise, or one close enough to something I had already planned for, there was a ready-made solution to fall back on. This was so much more manageable than trying to solve, and then memorise, every permutation of a rescue ahead of time, and over a few years I pulled together a number of different strategies. This wasn't too dissimilar in spirit to producing a series of go-to cooking recipes, or a list of DIY instructions. Having created a downloadable version, I made a printed version too, which would eventually become the blue folder. It has since prevented my brain from overthinking in rescues where a clear head was required.

EXPECT THE UNEXPECTED: THE CHECKLIST

- Avoid denial. Become comfortably uncomfortable.
- Expect curved balls. Be flexible.
- Go to the *Library Of Plans*. Borrow from the closest option.

LESSON #7

STEP UP AND STEP BACK

Learning when to take responsibility is a hugely important step as we become adults – it is one of the ways in which we're able to contribute effectively to a functioning society. (And problems often pile up when people don't take ownership of their actions.) It is also an essential part of being a cave diver. For example, I will always make sure to check and assemble my own equipment before an exploration or rescue. Leaving this to someone else – who might not be as conscientious as me – could be the difference between a successful dive and a disaster. But, exactly how we take ownership is just as important as committing to the act itself: we need to distinguish between taking rational and emotional responsibility, and understanding the indicators of both is a key skill . . .

DAYS SEVEN (PART THREE), EIGHT AND NINE
MONDAY 2 JULY – WEDNESDAY 4 JULY 2018

- - - - - - - - -

After the backslapping and congratulations for finding the Wild Boars (a fuss which made me feel very uncomfortable), the hard work began. To continue with our team-building efforts, Rick and I wanted to provide as full a debrief as possible to both the Thai and the American military teams in place. A meeting was set in the American encampment, a canvas-covered space just outside the cave entrance, and our information sharing took place later that night around a large trestle table where we were joined by various military figures. A number of other divers had joined the crowd, which only added to the pressure. Though matters weren't exactly helped when a member of a Chinese crew of divers placed a 360-degree camera in the middle of the table so he could record the event. I didn't have the energy to argue. Slumped in my chair, I was dog-tired.

Though the Americans were still realistic about the challenges ahead – as they had been throughout – a false sense of optimism had taken hold of the Thai Navy. Some of the rescuers thought that human ingenuity would save the day. Their attitude: *'Rescuing the Wild Boars is going be easy! We've put men on the moon, how difficult can it be to get a dozen kids out of a cave?'* But they had assumed, wrongly, that locating the kids represented 90 per cent of the problem and that the hard yards had been chalked off. Sadly, the numbers were pretty much back to front, and despite our small victory, we were still left with a daunting amount of work to tackle.

Hindsight is always twenty-twenty and crystal clear, but it seems to me that this overly optimistic mindset had been fuelled by the release of the video footage that I had shot inside the cave. My intention, in showing the kids waving to the camera, had been to provide proof of life to the authorities outside, as well as lifting the spirits of the people working on the ground, but the way in which the video was being presented on news stations and in viral clips worldwide seemed to suggest that a celebration was in order. For anyone watching at home, there was an assumption that the overall mission had almost been accomplished. *Job done!* Part of me regretted passing the camera up the chain of command so quickly.

'Perhaps I should have hung onto it until the official briefing had got underway?' I thought.

To paraphrase a line from the movie, *Top Gun*, I felt as if the Thai authorities had written a cheque they weren't entirely sure how to cash. A more sober take would have been to explain that the hard work hadn't yet started, and to underline this thought a grim, undisclosed truth was that many of the more realistic members of the rescue party were discussing just how many children might die during their extraction and what would be considered an acceptable mortality rate. One member of the US group even suggested that if we could save just one boy, our work could probably be considered a relative success, given that without our intervention they would all certainly die. Stats of that kind were thoroughly depressing.

It was at this point that I noticed the differing attitudes to responsibility opening up. Solo caving, particularly when diving alone, is the ultimate example of taking ownership because, really, the only person that can help if things go terribly wrong underwater is you. A rebreather fails? *You.* A mask gets damaged? *All you.* A tear appears in your wetsuit in icy cold water. *That's on you, too.* Alone, in the murk and the chill of churning, sediment-heavy currents, the responsibility for surviving or failing lies with only one person. And there's nobody else to blame if things go wrong, or the correct equipment for an unanticipated situation hasn't been brought into the cave.

But experience has taught me that it is actually possible to take one of two approaches to responsibility during a crisis, or indeed any situation – the rational and the emotional. The rational hinges upon acceptance and consideration: to acknowledge that the problem or issue is actually happening in the first place, and then to act carefully and without panic. The emotional tends to come to the fore when somebody ignores, or doesn't understand the full facts and evidence around them, and they then plunge headlong into a poorly thought-out plan of action.

From what I was seeing in the debrief, the first telltale signs of emotional responsibility were appearing. The most enthusiastic of the rescuers was Ben Reymenants. Almost from the minute the kids' survival had been announced, the Belgian seemed to be making grand gestures of bravado, even going so far as to suggest we should immediately launch a rescue attempt with only one stretcher. That simply couldn't have worked: 2.5kilometres (1.5 miles) of flooded passage separated us from chamber nine, and 1,500 metres (1,600 yards) of those were flooded. So far only Rick and I had been able to swim that distance.

Ben appeared to me to have also forgotten that one of the distinct facets of cave-rescue operations was caution and consideration. Much like a fire, or those shocked, panicked minutes and hours after an earthquake or explosion, every second counts, but a flooded cave, indeed any dangerous environment underwater, needs to be approached with care – swimming in recklessly can cost lives among the working divers; not thinking out the evacuation in advance might harm those marooned inside. Tham Luang was no different. I knew that without any real plan in place there was very little chance of getting the Wild Boars through the tunnels. The more appropriate approach was to take a moment, to think and to plan. Besides, we weren't running the rescue; the Thai military were, and by the looks of things they wanted to make the key decisions for themselves.

Ben wasn't having any of it, though. 'There are kids in there,' he insisted. 'We've got to go now!'

I argued my point, but Ben would not listen to reason until, eventually, I lost my rag. 'Either talk slower and sit down, or please leave,' I snapped.

Finally, he stormed off.

It seemed to me that Ben had allowed his emotions to overtake the situation. This was a strange reaction from an accomplished, technical dive instructor, but in his defence all of us were frazzled and exhausted. I know I was. Having been diving for nearly a week, the workload was taking its toll on my body and brain, and I felt shattered. I knew that I would have to take extra care when planning, communicating and operating at that point. I was fairly close to my limits, and it was highly likely that without caution I might make a mistake, especially given that I was almost delirious with fatigue and could barely stand. Arguing was the last thing I needed.

What happened next blindsided me: the Thais 'benched' both Rick and me, and at the end of the debrief, a representative from the Thai Navy thanked us both for our efforts and told us that we would be relegated to advisory positions. It felt crazy. We were probably the most experienced divers on the ground; we were certainly the only people who had been able to swim as far as chamber nine. I couldn't figure out what the hell had happened. *Was national pride dictating that Thai boys had to be saved by Thai military divers? Did they realise just how difficult the rescue would be?* I felt frustrated, and worried for the Wild Boars. It would not be long before the unpleasant realities of what laid ahead revealed themselves to everybody.

- - -

In the midst of all the chaotic planning and misguided optimism, a worrying snippet of information had made its way to the dive base. Four Thai Navy SEALs had become trapped in the ninth chamber, which included a medical expert called Dr Pak, who had been seconded to them for the duration of the mission. The hows and whys of what had happened still remain a mystery, but from what I could tell the team had gone in to check on the children, believing that by simply following our line, it would be possible for them to make the same round-trip of six hours. But they were wrong, and having used up way too much air on their way in they had been left with an unpleasant decision: leave immediately and risk death on the way out, or stay and hope for assistance – a predicament I had worked so hard to avoid during our last exploratory dive. They had gone for the latter and were stranded.

A second unit of Thai Navy divers had then swum into the depths of the cave to check on their wellbeing and found their comrades sitting on the bank alongside the kids in chamber nine. The most disappointing detail in this story, though, involved the food that had been taken into the cave during these trips. It seemed that the SEALs had transported in a small shipment of space blankets and energy gels to feed the boys, which sounded pretty underwhelming. When the Wild Boars' discovery was announced, much had been made of the foods they should, and should not be eating in their delicate condition. Higher-ups had declared that allowing them to consume 'normal meals' might cause certain medical issues, especially given that the boys had been starved for over a week. Even so, the nutrition they had been supplied with by the SEALs sounded incredibly insufficient.

The good news, though, was that the Wild Boars would at least have some company during the agonising days ahead. Certainly, the SEALs created an atmosphere of positivity among the group, which would only have added to a sense that everything was going to be OK. But still I fretted. *Surely those kids would need more than just an optimistic vibe, some space blankets and a bag of energy gels to stay alive?* Then I gloomily thought back to the dilemma we had experienced on finding the children, when we realised that the one chocolate bar Rick had stuffed into his sleeve wasn't going to be enough to feed thirteen people. Even dividing it among so many would have been problematic, and I had visualised a hellish situation as a small mob of starving children fought and brawled over a scrap of confectionery.

Slowly, the awful truth dawned on me. I said to Rick: 'Those kids are going to have to eat something substantial otherwise they'll be in trouble.'

In that moment, we decided to take ownership of something that *was* in our remit. We were going to swim into the ninth chamber with four large kit bags stuffed with ration packs supplied by the US Air Force, in order to give the Wild Boars their first nutritional meal in ten days. (If you could call it a meal. While it might have been nutritionally adequate, it hardly matched up to a plate of steaming pad thai.) Our only problem was that we had technically been 'grounded' by the authorities, and nobody had yet granted us permission to go back inside the cave.

Perhaps it was time to bend the rules. The US Air Force were on board with our idea, and helped us to prepare the rations by stripping away any unnecessary cardboard packaging. Most of the food would have to be transported wet, so items that were unlikely to survive the journey – such as crackers and teabags – were thrown out, too. We then made it clear to the Thai Navy what we intended to do and proceeded with our plan. They neither stood in our way, nor helped, but given we were taking responsibility for a pressing issue that very few people were prepared to acknowledge even existed, there was no reason for them to kick up a fuss.

When we swam through the cave to chamber nine, it would turn out to be my most taxing dive of the operation so far. The army kit bags I used to transport the ration packs were heavy and unwieldy. Usually, when carrying gear underwater, I liked to make sure of its buoyancy before swimming. Sometimes I would add foam to help with the process. Or, whenever we needed to add ballast to a bag, a lead weight, or even a handful of stones were used. In this case, we'd stuffed the pockets of what was a canvas bag with mud, but our efforts were a overzealous, and the extra load became too much. I was forced to drag the rations along like an anchor, kicking it up whenever I could with my legs, while attempting to follow the line. It made for exhausting work.

By the time I arrived at chamber six, a dark thought had crossed my mind.

'I'm going to use up all my air at this rate . . . Am I going to get stuck too?'

There were already seventeen individuals stranded in the belly of Tham Luang – the Wild Boars and four Thai Navy Seals. I really didn't want to add to the depressing numbers by remaining trapped inside. Having done some maths, I gestured to Rick that I was considering ditching one of the bags, in the hope that I would reduce my workload, and breathing, by hauling just the one package of food. I calculated there should still be sufficient rations inside to stave off the kids' hunger for a while. But Rick fixed me with a glare that needed little in the way of translation.

You're not dropping either of those bags. Fix the problem.

With some further determined poking and prodding, I managed to remove a little weight. I then strapped the bags together so they moved as one and I could swim ahead more comfortably.

A bizarre scene greeted us when we eventually emerged in chamber nine. A torch was being used to illuminate the inside of the cave, and on the bank there was a hubbub. The kids were playing with the Navy SEALs. A chequerboard had been scrawled with a stick into the sand, where a game of draughts was taking place with two sets of repurposed stones. It reminded me of a primary school set-up where the pupils engaged with their teacher in a fun, outdoors activity. Certainly, everybody inside seemed pleased to see us – the SEALs especially, who had been stuck inside for around twenty-four hours. (And because they probably understood the severity of their predicament better than the boys.) Our food delivery would go some way towards keeping the group alive. Though I reckoned we had transported a week's worth of supplies inside, I told the kids they had to make it last for two.

Much of the group's good mood probably stemmed from a sense of relief. We were able to tell the SEALs that their three colleagues had swum back without too much trouble. Then I passed on a sealed note that had been given to us by their commander, though we had been given strict instructions that we were not to read what was written inside. Rick watched them as they tore open the waterproof packet, sensing the orders that had been given.

'You're coming out last aren't you?' he said.

One of the SEALs nodded. They were not to leave the chamber until the boys had been brought back to safety. That meant that if Rick, myself, and the planners above ground, couldn't figure a way of transporting the boys, the SEALs would have to stay there, too, in which case they were highly like to die. But that wasn't the half of it. We had been instructed to swim in a package that was being referred to as a 'Special Communications Device', which, once unwrapped, turned out to be nothing more than an Android phone, a piece of kit that had next to no chance of functioning underground.

As we spoke to the kids and made to leave, more secretive notes were written in Thai and stuffed into the pouch. We were being treated as couriers and that annoyed me a bit. It was also hard not to feel a little anxious as to what was being communicated.

Our apprehensions only increased when we returned above ground and caught wind of the style of rescue being considered to move the mission forward. With the help of all the divers in attendance, including ourselves, the Thai Navy had decided that fifty or so SEALS, plus hundreds of air cylinders, were going to be strung throughout the tunnels in a human daisy chain. With this line stretched as far as chamber nine, each boy would then be passed through the flooded caverns and body-wide squeezes until they were planted safely on terra firma.

Having learned of the scheme, I felt dismayed. There simply weren't enough divers capable of making their way into the farthest reaches of the caverns, as the SEALs had already proved. Meanwhile, the very idea of passing the children back through Tham Luang via a daisy chain of people was a flight of fantasy. Some of the chambers were just too hazardous to hang around in. The plan was never going to work in a million years. Events only came to a head later that day when, during an informal gathering, a Thai official claimed that the situation was under control. As far as he was concerned, a solid scheme was taking shape. 'It's all going well,' he said, inaccurately.

I couldn't believe what I was overhearing. 'No, it's not,' I blurted out. 'The kids are completely fucked and they're all going to die.'

A murmur of shock rippled through the various members of management who were also present. As far as they were concerned, this was brand new information. They certainly hadn't heard anything, *anywhere* that suggested that the current plan wasn't anything other than the best option available. There were disgruntled murmurings. Though our discovery of the kids a day or so previously had seen our cramped quarters upgraded to salubrious, individual hotel rooms, Rick and I were still an unwanted presence. The Thai command did not want to hear that their plan was destined to fail, least of all from us.

Having delivered the unsettling news, our discussions with the Thai authorities continued until gradually, with a little more planning and re-planning, we agreed that the rescue mission could be streamlined further by reducing the numbers of personnel and equipment involved. (With the help of the American Air Force we then reduced them some more.) Finally, the Thai command decided that Rick and I would have to lead the rescue. They realised that nobody else gathered at the entrance of Tham Luang could swim such a number of trapped kids to safety through around 1,500 metres (1,600 yards) of flooded tunnels, though we were hardly relaxed about the task in hand ourselves. The challenges were so much bigger than anything else we had experienced before. For starters, how would we safely execute such a gruelling mission, especially when it was highly likely that the kids would be terrified and panicked as we pushed them through the water or flooded caves? And what would happen if some of them died under our care?

Those heavy details, when they were eventually discussed, would leave me feeling more than a little uncomfortable. But for now, at least, we were stepping up.

OWNING IT IN THE REAL WORLD

One of the most powerful tools when taking responsibility is honesty and when facing up to a challenge, we can use it in a number of ways.

So, for example . . .

Honesty of strength: If you are the most able first aider in the group of friends on a hiking trip, take responsibility for administering any medical assistance should it be required.

Honesty of weakness: if your GCSE in Spanish was taken twenty years ago, maybe leave the food ordering to a more linguistically capable friend during a holiday abroad.

Honesty of situation: when things are going horribly wrong, or you're feeling out of your depth in a work project, ask for help, or advice.

Honesty of consequences: if you're going to participate in a sport as dangerous as base-jumping, adopting the 'it-won't-happen-to-me' mindset serves as a flimsy insurance policy. Accept there are risks involved.

Honesty of action: after making a mistake that carries implications for others, own up to it as soon as possible.

I was faced with that very situation after returning from our first food run into the cave. Having deposited my two kit bags of ration packs in chamber nine, I made the heavy return journey to the entrance only to become tangled up in an underwater spider's web of black wire, much of which had been laid in the days before the cave had fully flooded. At that time, the Thai Navy SEALs were attempting to set up a telephone line throughout Tham Luang and I remember thinking then it was just one of a handful of unlikely operations that were being discussed.

Nevertheless, the long shot that it might be possible to communicate via phone inside the tunnels seemed too good to resist, and given the work had gone on regardless, I had no way of knowing whether the cable that held me fast was now unused, or the focus of some ongoing effort. I attempted to wriggle free from the tangle, but it was no good; the wire was irreversibly wound round my leg. My only route out was to cut sightlessly through the wire with my shears. Now free, I continued towards chamber three and the dive base, wrestling with the implications of my actions. Part of me wanted to put my head in the sand, to pretend that it hadn't really happened.

Do I say something? Do I not say something? I might have really fucked up here . . .

I then realised that other divers were possibly swimming into Tham Luang to lay more wire, risking their lives in the process. If a communication line was eventually established, but a malfunction caused by my incident was discovered, somebody would then have to figure out the cause of the problem. A process of that kind could potentially last for days. In the end, I knew I had to do the right thing and admit to my actions.

'This is what I've done. This is where the break is,' I confessed, 'I can go back in and fix it.'

It turned out that the project had been abandoned, but at least I could rest easily, knowing I had done the right thing.

For example, when signing a mobile phone or credit card contract many people adopt the position that life's too short to read the small print. They argue that it's several pages of boring and complicated legalese and that there are more productive ways of spending their time. But that's why so many people get a shock several months down the line when they discover that they have unwittingly committed to an expensive package, or have locked themselves into an automatic upgrade by mistake. This lazy part of our nature can be so strong that we need to make the effort to retrain our brains. One way of doing so is to focus on the small, fiddly things in everyday life that we can affect, simply by taking responsibility. Such as reading that contract in full. Or checking our insurance hasn't run out. Or making sure our passport has a couple of years on it when booking the next holiday, and so on . . .

The cave diving equivalent to this scenario was highlighted to me during an exploration in the Jura region of France. I was lucky enough to have the backing of a number of French divers who had agreed to provide support by staging equipment at various points throughout the cave. Having other team members position equipment this way can save a tremendous amount of effort. Still, wherever possible, I'm always careful not to commit myself to a dive without ensuring all the equipment needed for a safe exit is in place. In this case, my support team experienced significant difficulties reaching their pre-agreed drop-off points. On following them in, I became involved in a game of underwater *I-Spy*, as I tried to spot and retrieve the equipment that had been dumped almost at random throughout the early sections of the cave because my support divers weren't able to carry it through.

Incidents of this kind only highlight what have long been personal rules: I always try to take responsibility for myself. I do my best to act with honesty. And I always read the small print. As a result, I know that if I do come to a sticky end when working underwater, there will be nobody else to blame but me.

STEP UP AND STEP BACK: THE CHECKLIST

- Take ownership. Accept responsibility.
- Be realistic. Don't overreach.
- Play to your strengths. Acknowledge your weaknesses.

LESSON #8

HARNESSING TEAMWORK AND TRUST

The concept of trust is a mortal one in cave diving, as it would be in a dangerous vocation such as firefighting. When working in a group, every diver places their life in the hands of others, so it's important that he, or she knows without any doubt that their colleagues can be relied upon. Those connections are often hard to find, or they might take years to establish, which is why Rick Stanton and I have worked so well together in the past. Decades of diving as a duo have created a firm bond – he has my back and I have his. But in order to create trust within a group setting, it's vital the people working in the collective understand the key elements of teamwork – the sharing of information, collective thinking, the power of controlled ego and the distribution of credit. Only then can they operate together successfully . . .

DAYS EIGHT AND NINE
TUESDAY 3 JULY—WEDNESDAY 4
JULY 2018

- - - - - - - - -

This was shaping up to be the most complex rescue mission I had ever worked on. Thankfully, our efforts were being supported by a collection of military and civilian specialists from Australia, America and Thailand, among others – individuals who were both skilled and effective. However, what was really needed were divers I had worked with previously; people I could trust, because without a strong team connection I would eventually find myself fixed in a constant state of high alert as I worked underwater, worrying about whatever Diver A was doing, or whether Diver B had staged our cylinders in the correct spot. My focus needed to remain at all times on the kids, not to mention on my own safety.

Before we could think about adding to our numbers on the ground, I first had to improve our relations with the local armed forces. While we had undoubtedly established a bond with the Americans, our biggest logistical obstruction was still proving to be the Thai Navy SEALs, or, at least, their superiors. We were constantly being made to feel like an inconvenience, despite our key role in the rescue; but I felt that their cooperation, however difficult to secure, was essential. As a planning team made of Rick and myself, plus senior members of the US Air Force, figured out how best to manoeuvre thirteen people from the ninth chamber, any suggestions from us were dismissed by the authorities; any requests we made were still being greeted with indifference. A strange tension was developing, which I tried to overcome by communicating the details of our plans to the Navy SEALs whenever it seemed appropriate.

Simultaneously, we contacted the British Embassy in Bangkok. It had become clear to us that the divers Jason Mallinson and Chris Jewell, plus support personnel Gary Mitchell and Mike Clayton needed to be working alongside us, as they were people that Rick and I had respected and trusted for years. Jason and Chris were long-term dive partners who I had worked with multiple times over the years – I swam alongside Jason on our record-breaking exploration in Pozo Azul. Importantly, both were dived up and carried a decade or two of experience in exploring cave-diving terrain similar to the kind we were working through in Tham Luang.

Meanwhile, Mike and Gary were experienced surface controllers. Their role would be to manage everything above ground, which included liaising with the military, coordinating our equipment supplies, and fending off the media. The dive team of Rick and myself, plus Jason and Chris, would be underwater for many hours without any form of contact with surface control. (Conventional radio and smart phone signals simply do not function underground, or underwater.) Mike and Gary would know exactly what to do in those silent hours.

The arrival of all four was arranged in two waves through the British Cave Rescue Council and the Thai embassy in the UK. Jason and Chris showed up within two days, Mike and Gary followed shortly after. We requested the help of three more divers: Josh Bratchley, Jim Warny and Connor Roe. Apparently,

Josh had been abroad when our message for additional assistance had come through and he was flown home and then back to the airport again, a police escort steering him the whole way, its blue lights flashing. Connor was more prepared, having prepared and packed his gear in anticipation of a phone call.

Rick and I were now working with a group of divers we both knew and trusted. Teamwork and communication would be key, as would our ability to encourage our new teammates to *want* to succeed as much as we did, because I had developed an incredibly strong sense of ownership of the kids' wellbeing and I intended to work to the limits of my personal safety in order to save them. Perhaps irrationally, I believed that nobody was going to commit to the job in the same way as me, though I also understood the impossibility of being a control freak in such a huge operation. More than anything, I felt it was important to give ourselves the best shot at success, no matter what it took.

When selecting a team such as the one we were building in Tham Luang, I had found that it's most important to choose people that I have trusted in the past and then to trust the people I choose. As far as I'm concerned, the perfect dive group is one where every individual within it is responsible for their roles, they can operate competently on their own, they are able to look after themselves, and finally, they possess enough capacity and discipline to assist a team-mate or a casualty, especially if disaster strikes. Beyond that, it's important that everybody is happy to work as part of a team and then functions in a selfless manner. Egotism, as I'll discuss later, is a troubling trait in a cave diver.

Overall, though, trust is the most important attribute when working as a team underwater and with it, Rick and I have saved each other's lives several times. On one occasion, in southern

France during 2007, he was eager to dive into unexplored passages in a cave located in Saint-Sauveur, in the Dordogne region. The two of us, plus another diver, Rupert Skorupka, had planned to dive separately. On the first day, Rupert and I swam into the furthest known reaches of the cave, familiarising ourselves with the terrain while being supported by Rick. The next day, we swapped with Rick as he attempted to push into unknown territory.

In many ways, we were breaking new ground, technologically speaking. In 2007, it was considered unusual, perhaps even risky, to dive to some of the depths we'd planned for while using rebreathers. There simply hadn't been enough successful cave dives with the equipment we were using to draw conclusions as to which of our procedures would be safe. Rick was aiming to push past 180 metres (200 feet), a depth that was nearly twice as deep as that reached by the ill-fated Russian submarine, the *Kursk* when it had sunk in 2000.

But very little had been written on how to achieve those numbers, not without the logistical support that commercial divers enjoyed*, and we felt that a much more lightweight approach was required. Rick and I had decided to use a different type of rebreather at depth, one we hoped would prevent a lethal build-up of carbon dioxide in our system. We had also developed what we believed were suitable plans and procedures to integrate

---

* Commercial divers or 'saturation divers', such as those working on oil rigs can spend many days in a pressurised environment. They operate from diving bells and have teams of surface support personnel managing their wellbeing; they are always connected to the diving bell by a life support umbilical cord or hose, and have huge banks of oxygen and other gases on hand for emergency purposes. This type of infrastructure simply isn't possible in exploration dives, or the type of rescues I was engaged in, mainly due to the huge expense. The small size and location of most caves was a prohibitive factor too. (Though one exception was the Wakulla 2 Expedition in Florida in 1998, where a diving bell was used to make the hours of decompression more comfortable.)

our rebreathers with the equipment and dive computers we already had. All things considered, it was very much a work in progress.

My first dive was thankfully uneventful. Having reached a depth of around 130 metres (425 feet), I swam over a kilometre (over half a mile) into the cave. *And the rebreather had worked!* But Rick's exploration the following morning was far more colourful. As a support diver, I was required to meet him a couple of hours into the exploration, during his decompression, where I would then help to remove any unwanted equipment while providing moral support. But on making it 250 metres (800 feet) into the cave, I saw no sign of him at the rendezvous point. I ventured another several hundred metres inside, but there was still no sign. An uneasy feeling clawed at my gut. Hours passed; I returned to the surface for air and then made a second fruitless dive but I still couldn't spot Rick anywhere. It was only on my third attempt that I eventually, *thankfully*, located him. He had spent much longer at depth than expected, and though his emotions were in check, he was clearly unhappy. Despite a successful exploration, Rick had used more gas than expected and his breathable supply wasn't likely to last for very long into decompression. He was in a bit of a fix.

Rick wears a black mask, and underwater he has an uncanny ability to deliver a withering stare, usually when the person alongside him is about to do something stupid. I was now on the receiving end of that look. Gesturing me close, Rick asked for my underwater notebook and I wondered what the hell I had done wrong. When he eventually turned the waterproof pages my way, four words had been scrawled on the surface in pencil.

I NEED YOUR REBREATHER.

The demand was unsettling. Divers simply don't exchange gear underwater, especially several hundred meters into a cave, and definitely not at the significant depths we'd found ourselves in. Though I was undoubtedly questioning, I trusted Rick and knew he wouldn't have asked me had he not thought a) it was necessary and b) there was no other choice. Another glare left me in little doubt that we were fast approaching crunch point, while at the same time suggesting that the request was completely normal and could be accommodated by just about any fool. (It's funny what just one look can tell you.) I composed myself and then indicated I would need around a minute to fashion a make-shift harness for my cylinders, one that would allow me to exit the cave without my rebreather. Rick was staring again.

You can have a minute . . . but no longer.

As we began the complex process of exchanging equipment, Rupert Skorupka entered the water to see what was happening. As he swam into view, I noticed his eyes. They had been magnified by his dive mask and were as wide as a pair of saucers. To him the scene must have looked like some kind of madness: enough equipment to start a dive school had been strewn all about the passage. Above him, Rick was calmly floating at the ceiling; I was below, lying on the floor, and both of us were adjusting our equipment without actually wearing any of it.

As Rick fiddled with my rebreather, I realised he'd never worked with that particular model before, and therefore had no idea how it might function, not that quibbling over this particular fact seemed very sensible at the time. Furthermore, what I didn't know (and wouldn't discover until surfacing) was that Rick's rebreather had failed and was fast filling with water. We swapped kits and I delivered a brief lesson on his new rebreather unit, distilling the bare essentials of several days' worth of teaching into around ninety seconds. Having got the message, he visibly relaxed and began what would be twelve, long, lonely hours of underwater decompression. With the immediate problem solved, I swam Rick's rebreather to the surface, where I drained away the water inside, replaced the carbon dioxide absorbent and recharged the oxygen cylinders. I then returned it to Rick, whereupon Rupert and I could set about helping him through the night as he continued his slow ascent in stages.

Despite the drama, Rick's exploration of Saint-Sauveur had been successful, because we had trusted each other implicitly. We were a small but effective team. Over ten years later in Tham Luang, the scale of our task demanded a far bigger workforce, and in addition to Jason, Chris, Mike and Gary, we needed a team of support divers to help us set equipment throughout the cave. After Ben Reymenants and his dive partner had departed and a new group of European diving instructors working in Southern Thailand had arrived. Among them were Claus Rasmussen and Ivan Karadzic (both from Denmark), Mikko Paasi (from Finland), and Erik Brown (from Canada). The positive side of their arrival was that the number of technical divers working on the ground had expanded; and given they were also expats living in the south of Thailand, they understood the area and the culture. The negative was that none of them had any experience in working on cave rescues.

When the US Air Force first introduced the group, and insisted we work with them, I was wary. But over the coming days, we assessed their suitability through a series of tasks that would prepare the caverns for the upcoming rescue – they moved lines through the tunnels, tidied up the cave of equipment and discarded cylinders, and cut away some of the inactive wires that had been blocking our path in some of the sumps. We soon nicknamed our new recruits the 'Euro Divers'.

These were relatively low-priority chores. If one of the Euro Divers cocked up, or failed to complete their work, it was of no great consequence, but any blunder would shine a light on who was capable and who wasn't. We had to know which guys delivered on their promises and which ones fell short. Some of the Euro Divers only went into the cave once before deciding the work was not for them. The egotists in the group were noted too. In much the same way that a new line manager likes to assess the staff working around them in a company during their first few weeks in the job, so we were assessing our resources, only we had minutes and hours in which to make that assessment, rather than days and weeks. After several shifts of work, Claus and Mikko proved to be very helpful indeed – they hadn't died and were more than prepared to swim into the caves, over and over. They seemed competent and in control, and I felt confident working alongside them. Both divers would turn out to be useful additions.

The team was in place. Rick and I, plus Jason and Chris would work as lead divers. Mike and Gary were set to run all above-ground communications and logistics, while a mixed team featuring the likes of Josh, Connor, Mikko and Claus would act as support divers, staging air cylinders and other equipment throughout the cave. At various stages we would also rely on members of the American Air Force and Australian Navy. A comprehensive plan wasn't yet in place, but at least we had the crew to tackle the workload ahead.

BEWARE THE EGO

There is little room for ego when exploring caves, though plenty of divers carry one with them and the sport is a magnet for big personalities. But competitive bravado can lead to reckless behaviour and pig-headedness, which can cause all manner of unpleasant scenarios. One of the reasons I've worked well with others is because I have never attempted to compete; proving myself to the people around me isn't my thing. Instead, I am competitive with myself and I am a harsh self-critic. Yet when it comes to presenting myself as an authority figure I'm just not interested.

There was one occasion when my attitude became very apparent. I was diving into a cave in southern France with a colleague called 'David', an experienced cave and commercial diver who was a very accomplished explorer. (For the purposes of this story, I have changed his identity.) David would need all his famed nerve as this cave had a very tricky profile: the passages led us down to depths of around 100 metres (325 feet) before rising up again, and then down, and up, and down again. *It was like a bloody roller coaster.* In decompression terms, this dive was considered a very risky exploration.

For this particular trip, we had decided to work as a parallel team, meaning that if one of us turned back for any reason, the other would still continue forwards, and we eventually made it out of the water and into an area of previously unexplored cave. Up until that moment, neither of us had discussed what we should do in the event of breaking new ground, and having got to the point where we were clearly about to do so, I realised the route ahead looked sketchy and that we should tread carefully.

We were faced with a 45-degree rock slope that rose out of the water, with a number of dangerous looking drops on the left side. The only way on was to crawl up the slope and then along the tortuously low passage beyond. If one, or both of us, was to become trapped or injured, I knew of very few divers in the world with the ability to rescue us. (And the expense of the amount of beer I'd have to buy Rick, if he was called into action, didn't bear thinking about.)

Then there was the issue of our kit. Both of us were carrying plenty of it, and as we squeezed through a narrow tube in the rock, hoping it would lead into another cavern rather than wedging us tightly inside, the smallest of movements made for heavy work. We had also been wearing drysuits, because the water temperature was freezing cold, but with so much physical effort now taking place out of the water, I realised I was overheating; my skin was covered in sweat, a situation that meant the dive back would be extremely chilly, not to mention the hours spent in decompression afterwards.[*]

Meanwhile, the terrain we were crawling over was strewn with jagged rocks. (Unexplored cave passages are often made up of razor-sharp stone, because nobody has clambered over them, to smooth the surfaces.) The slightest tear to a drysuit would have made it impossible for the wearer to swim back – as I've discussed previously, just the slightest nick would have exposed the diver's skin to a brutally cold underwater environment. To say we were taking a risk at this stage in the exploration was an understatement.

---

[*] Drysuits keep out the water, but when a cave diver is soaked with sweat, the thermal layers underneath become damp. In icy temperatures, hanging around in wet garments can lead to hypothermia.

But David wanted to be the first into the next stretch of water, to make his mark on the cave. Or at least, that's how it looked to me. As we continued our exploration, he surged ahead, still carrying his kit with him. Suddenly, an awful realisation dawned upon me.

'He wants to go first. He wants to go the furthest. *He's bloody charging ahead!*'

It wasn't a game I wanted to play. And as I watched David rushing on, a showreel of potential disasters played out in my head. By carrying so much kit at speed, over this unstable terrain, he could easily fall, twist an ankle or break an arm.

And then . . . *near disaster!*

While scaling a muddy bank, he slipped. David's backside slid out from underneath him and he skidded and tumbled down the gradient for around 10 metres (30 feet) before landing in a pool of water. It was a relief to see him unhurt, but I understood even more clearly that rushing in an environment of this kind was foolhardy. What had mattered to me was that we succeeded as a team. I certainly wasn't exploring this cave for personal glory, and I had no real desire to be the first one past whatever imaginary finishing line lay ahead.

I had long known that one technique for preventing a big personality – even an overbearing ego – from imploding is to slow the down the situation they are working in. During a business meeting setting, for example, a work colleague might become too confrontational, or appear eager to press ahead with an idea that others in the team are unsure of, or resistant to. In those instances it helps to take a break, or to call a timeout to slow the pace of a situation that might otherwise quickly spiral out of control. I had to employ a similar tactic with David.

In desperation, I called out, hoping to simmer him down a little. 'Wait! I'll carry your equipment for you,' I shouted.

The shift in our momentum was almost instantaneous. David, suddenly stripped of any competition, dropped gears, knowing that he would be the first diver into the next sump or chamber. Having shared his load between us and settled what had looked to me like a race, we successfully found and explored the next sump without too much drama.

Taking the backseat in a team environment is often the best tactic to adopt when a bullish personality is determined to drive everybody forwards at any cost. That's not to say we should become passive, or blindly follow a reckless or overly ambitious leader. Instead, we should use our influence to control the situation subtly, so that everybody feels pleased with the eventual outcome. Often, I have likened this situation to working on an old sailing ship, where a strong character, absolutely determined to lead the way, takes charge as captain.

Having expressed a determination to steer, and knowing that the direction is roughly the correct one, it helps if the other crew members are willing to park their egos, working around the big personality in question in such a way that the overall objective is achieved satisfactorily. As the self-appointed captain presses forward, his crew should keep an eye on what is happening at the side of the vessel, or check the compass, and scan the horizon for other boats. Really, there's no need for the others to attempt to stamp their authority on a situation while the ship is heading in the right direction. And if, for some reason, start taking a turn for the worse, the attentive crew will be the first to know. From there, they can work through the issues in play with their captain.

Too often, the opposite happens; a team of personalities, unhappy at being led, or at having their egos challenged, clash in such a way that an ugly power struggle breaks out. I have seen this all too often when watching the reality TV show, *The Apprentice*. During the weekly group challenges, where a number of hopefuls attempt to catch Lord Alan Sugar's eye with their creative business acumen, a hierarchy is often arranged in advance; one contestant is installed at random as team leader. But what happens next is often the exact opposite to what should occur on my imagined ship. Crew members rarely check the sides of the boat. No one takes responsibility for the compass. The horizon is left unchecked. Instead a war of personalities kicks off in which the more egotistical members of the group vie for leadership, while undermining any potential successes they might have shared. It is a complete waste of time for everyone, though there's no denying it makes for entertaining TV.

Interestingly, there is a technique for those leaders who know they have a big personality (and also those without one), and it can be used to overcome any simmering tension their ego might be causing. It is well known that one of the key traits of an alpha character is the overwhelming desire to take charge, or to lead in whatever's going on, whether that be in sport, a social activity, business or sometimes family life. However, in those environments, when feelings can be hurt and plans can be derailed, one way for leaders to create respect and understanding is by simply sharing the credit within the group whenever success comes their way. In the case of *The Apprentice*, any team leader that publicly acknowledges the efforts of their teammates – the ones who so ably contributed to the overall work – will find their colleagues more agreeable to helping out next time around. Likewise, taking one for the team, or accepting responsibility when things don't work out as planned is often repaid with respect and loyalty.

There have been situations where I have been forced to take the lead, and I've found this same technique to be very helpful when bringing a team together. For example, while working in Tham Luang, our dive team received requests to give media interviews. During the rescue, we firmly refused. Afterwards, however, during conversations with journalists, we generally made sure to stress that our efforts to save the Wild Boars had been conducted as an 'International Team'. Deflecting the credit away from individuals and pushing it towards the group seemed a good way of making sure that everyone's contributions were acknowledged.

It was a technique I tried to use after the rescue, when our group of motley divers was invited to Downing Street to meet with the former prime minister, Theresa May. Sadly, Rick was unable to make it and the responsibility for explaining the events that had unfolded in Tham Luang was placed firmly on my shoulders. Throughout the conversation, I made sure to introduce the others in the team and then to spread the credit equally among the group. To my frustration, Mrs May continually fired the attention back at me, until our chat resembled a tennis rally, though I think my teammates appreciated the effort. (The undoubted highlight of the visit was watching Matthew, my twelve-year-old son and guest for the day, as he sat in the PM's chair in the Cabinet Room like he owned the place. He then polished off more than his fair share of cake.) As a person, I'm generally validated internally, and though I like the respect of my peers, I don't *need* it. I have always felt that respect and trust are earned, rather than bought, or built by bullying. As far as I'm concerned, leaders achieve much better results by under-promising and over-delivering, by being respectful and reliable, and by working towards a group goal. It is not vital for them to always steer the ship – or grab the glory.

HARNESSING TEAMWORK AND TRUST: THE CHECKLIST

- Select those you trust. Trust those you select.
- Share information. Respect viewpoints.
- Delegate responsibility. Steer only when necessary.

LESSON #9

HURRY UP AND DO . . . *NOTHING*

Sometimes when a crisis situation develops around us, it's tempting to want to rush into action and to fix things. (And to fix things now!) However, the reality is that some crisis events play out like a game of chess in which rushing headlong into a poorly thought-out plan of attack, or defence, can be the worst thing to do – mistakes are made, key pieces are lost and accidents happen along the way. Through rushing we find ourselves manoeuvred into checkmate.

Instead, it's sometimes better that we hurry up and . . . do nothing. I know this sounds counter-intuitive, but by pausing for breath in the first three seconds of a dispute, accident, or failed plan (see Lesson #5), or by making a little room to think in a situation where the clock isn't against us, we can plot our escape away from trouble, all the while using haste rather than speed . . .

DAYS TEN AND ELEVEN
THURSDAY 5 JULY—FRIDAY 6 JULY 2018

Tragedy had struck.

I could tell something was wrong as soon as we arrived at the entrance to the cave that morning. The mood was subdued; the emotional impetus had faded, and there was very little evidence of the enthusiasm created by the discovery of the Wild Boars just a couple of days earlier. *But what the hell had happened?* Having spoken to a handful of engineers around us, the grim truth about the dangers of cave diving was confirmed. One of the rescuers, a former Thai Navy SEAL named Saman Gunan, had died somewhere in Tham Luang. The news came as a terrible blow.

From what I knew about Saman, he was aged thirty-eight, an athletic bloke, and physically capable enough to cope with the rigours of a gruelling penetration into the caves. However, superior physical fitness counted for very little when negotiating a flooded passage or managing the air supply required for a round trip over 1.5 kilometres (a mile) underground. It was the latter that had scuppered Saman, and during the return leg, tragically, he had run out of air and drowned. Perhaps a lack of recent experience had been the vital factor: Saman was a volunteer, and having left the Thai Navy SEALs in 2006, he had gone on to work as a patrol officer at Bangkok's Suvarnabhumi Airport. That hadn't diminished his enthusiasm for an against-all-odds challenge, though, and after learning of the Wild Boars' predicament, he had decided to help with the rescue efforts.

While the exact order of events and some of the details surrounding his death are a mystery, the broader outlines of what had happened sounded sadly familiar to anyone associated with cave diving. Saman had swum to some of the deeper reaches of the cave, beyond chamber five, with a haul of oxygen cylinders. By the sounds of things, there hadn't been too many problems on the way in. But on the return trip, his dive buddy turned around to check that everything was OK, only to find Saman had slipped into unconsciousness. First aid was delivered and Saman was transported to dive base in chamber three, where he was given CPR, but nothing could be done. He was gone. After Governor Narongsak relayed the news to the workforce at Tham Luang, the buzz and optimism that had been charging through the camp fizzed away like a sigh of air from a punctured tyre.

A great deal of speculation can swirl around during the frantic hours and days following a diver's death. *Could anything have been done differently to prevent Saman's accident? Was his equipment at fault? Had he misread the measurements on his cylinder contents gauge?* These curiosities are usually put to rest by a thorough investigation of the incident, but any information that might have been drawn from such an investigation wasn't shared. I found that a little unsettling. If, for example, Saman's drowning had been caused by a bad air fill, one that contained carbon monoxide from the compressor exhaust, then a wider problem might have been in play: his tank could have been one of a bad batch of air cylinders, meaning every diver on site was playing a worrying game of Russian roulette as they inhaled from their regulators. However, the most logical assessment was that Saman had died having run out of air. I felt desperately sad for his friends and family, and it was yet another reminder of the high stakes nearly constantly at hand.

We had to move on; there was no time to dwell on the loss. Part of our work now involved familiarising our newly assembled dive team, which included Jason, Chris, Jim and the Euro Divers, with the deeper recesses of Tham Luang, and there was plenty to learn. Swimming into chambers three, four and five was one thing. Getting to the final cavern was an entirely different kettle of fish, and it would take nerve, stamina and skill to get there. Our new arrivals were fresh and physically up to the task, but I worried that the difficulty of the rescue and the involvement of children could create an emotional fallout if things went wrong – I had noticed that with each run into the ninth cavern, our connection with both the boys and the SEALs was growing. Sometimes, I found it hard to detach myself psychologically from what could prove to be a very painful and depressing conclusion. The thought of any of the kids dying, especially one that might have been directly in my care, was deeply concerning. If there was a chance I could minimise any potential mental anguish for my teammates, I was eager to do so. (Though cave divers aren't renowned for sharing their inner thoughts. We can be a pretty closed-off bunch.)

I was most concerned for Chris. Behind Rick, Jason and myself, he was the most experienced diver on the ground, even though he was yet to prove himself in a real rescue. For this reason, it was important he familiarised himself with the cave before the extraction of the Wild Boars got underway. He wanted to meet the kids, but I worried that his enthusiasm had caused him to overlook the potential emotional consequences. With hindsight, I don't think he understood the grim seriousness of what he was getting into, and by swimming into chamber nine in advance, he was only going to bond with a group of people who had a very slim chance of surviving the eventual rescue operation. I guess his emotions might have been running hot. As an officer with British Cave Rescue Council, he had become a spokesperson on the Tham Luang rescue at home. Now transported to Thailand and part of the team for real, he was eager to pull his weight and prove his worth.

At one point, Rick even asked Chris if he was certain of his actions. 'If you go in, you might be one of the last to see these children alive,' he said. 'Are you sure that's what you want?'

Chris nodded and pressed on into the cave with Jason for their first run. I watched him go, hoping he wouldn't come to regret the experience.

In the end, both divers were able to make it to the Wild Boars without too much incident. And having handed over the latest run of supplies, they decided to hatch another plan. A series of notes, written by the kids' parents, had been carried in with the ration packs. While watching the boys' faces as they read through their letters, every missive full of love and support and hope, Jason wondered if there was any value in encouraging the Wild Boars to reciprocate the gesture. Handing over a pencil, he instructed everybody to scribble down replies of their own. His hope was that their words might lift the spirits of the frazzled families waiting outside.

The pages brimmed with optimism. All the children told their parents they loved them; others spoke of being excited at leaving the caves. Titan even placed a dinner order for when he eventually made it home. 'Please tell Pee Yod, get ready to take me to eat fried chicken.'

'I am fine,' wrote Dom. 'It is a bit cold, but don't worry. Please don't forget my birthday.'

Coach Ek put together a note in which he told his grandmother not to worry, before pencilling an apology to the families expressing his sorrow at the Wild Boars' predicament: *To all kids' parents, at this moment, kids are well. They have team work who are bigger to take care of them. I promise you that I will do my best to take care of them. I would like to thank you for moral support and I apologise to all parents.* Given the age of the kids stuck in the cave, it was easy to forget that at twenty-five, Ek had not long been a grown-up himself.

While the letters were certainly morale-boosting, our team had a job to do, and we had to do it well. I needed to shut out any external white noise and focus on the task in hand, but the reconnaissance effort brought a new message from the military trapped inside. The four SEALs had claimed they could hear the sound of snorting pigs and squawking chickens from the depths of Tham Luang. Drawing from that incredibly flimsy evidence, the Thai authorities began to direct their attention towards any farms that were located in the area. Their hope was that an open shaft might be found somewhere above chamber nine. After all, what else could explain those farm-yard animal noises ricocheting into the caves?

But life underground can be a disorientating experience, especially for someone who has been trapped in very uncomfortable circumstances for days. Lights will flash and flicker in the distance, even though there is nobody else around. As water flows through the tunnels it's also possible to hear strange noises and voices, sometimes as murmurs – sentences and names that echo eerily through the darkness. Each one raises the hope that help is on its way, but they are usually nothing more than a false dawn. The experience isn't too dissimilar to those excitable moments spent waiting for a mate, or a loved one, at a train station on a gloomy winter evening. Every face or silhouette that walks through the ticket office as the latest commuter train pulls in – their collars turned up, hands shoved into pockets – can resemble the person you're waiting for until the truth is revealed from a distance of 30 metres (100 feet) or so. Hundreds of people turn out to be nothing more than a false promise.

But hearing things is totally normal in a cave. Divers understand this reality; stranded and scared individuals with no real experience of operating underground rarely do, and so the Thai military had become convinced that a search should be made for some imagined menagerie of livestock when all that was above the Wild Boars was a vast expanse of jungle and nearly a kilometre (over half a mile) of mountain rock.

My best course of action was to wait and prepare – *and to hurry up and do nothing*. It seemed like the smartest choice under the circumstances. From my perspective, all that could be done was being done. Chris and Jason were familiarising themselves with the cave and taking in supplies. The Euro Divers were working on their own preparations; the equipment we needed was being sourced and readied; and our infrastructure was coming together nicely. Any fussing or micro-management on my part wasn't going to help. Alongside Rick, I took a moment to rest and recover, and then to ready the best possible plan to rescue those kids.

THERE'S NO SUCH THING AS A ZERO-RISK OPTION

As we went to work on figuring out just how we were going to extract the Wild Boars, Governor Narongsak had made a bold proclamation. When it came to any suggestion tabled by the various rescue teams, he would only accept a 'zero-risk plan'. By that, I took it to mean that if there were the slightest chance that somebody might die during the process – whether that person be a SEAL, a diver, or a Wild Boar – then the operation would be scrapped and the brainstorming would begin again. I remember rolling my eyes on hearing his announcement. Every action in life, let alone in a cave rescue, comes with some form of risk attached.

There was also the reality of our situation to consider. Given there was no such thing as a Zero Risk Option available in cave rescues, the children would theoretically have had to remain inside chamber nine until the waters had subsided. But we were in the early phases of monsoon season; that meant the kids and the SEALs having to live in Tham Luang for months. Given the Thai's military dive teams were unable to swim to chamber nine and back with anything approaching consistency, the food distribution system would probably break down at some point and the kids would eventually starve, though the sanitation in the cave was going to cause all manner of serious health problems long before then. In that respect, the Zero Risk Option carried the likelihood of a 100 per cent mortality rate.

Many actions in life involve some form of risk. Crossing the road. Chopping onions. Getting on a plane. None of these processes are inherently *risky*, but to assume none of them present any potential consequences whatsoever is incredibly naïve. We might step into the road, unthinking, and walk into the path of a speeding bus. While chopping onions, our super-sharp knife might slip and cause a terrible injury. I won't go into the potential risks of flying just in case anyone reading this is phobic, but there are plenty of Hollywood films that depict the worst-case scenarios, should you wish to go there.

Strangely, as a society, we seem to have forgotten that everything we do in life carries risks – both big and small. When a serious car accident happens, or a gas explosion takes place, bold statements are made. *This must never be allowed to happen again.* Sometimes overzealous safety measures are installed in the aftermath. But continuing that line of thinking to its logical conclusion would see us banning cars (there were 1,580 road traffic deaths in the UK during the year ending June 2020) and cutting off domestic gas supplies in the home. Sober reality requires us to accept that those risks exist. Then it's up to us to acknowledge which threats we feel are acceptable, and then work to mitigate them as best we can.

When crossing the road, actually take the time to look as well as listen.

When chopping onions with a very sharp knife, cut along a line that's away from the body.

When settling into your plane seat, watch the safety instruction video instead of flicking through the movie menu. (That can wait for five minutes, surely?)

These are simple precautions. And rather than living in a constant state of ignorance at one end of the spectrum, and hyper-anxiety at the other, we can learn to accept the consequences of our actions. Most of all, we should forget the concept of the Zero Risk Option.

It simply doesn't exist.

LET THE SEDIMENT SETTLE

For Rick and myself, the very act of doing nothing – other than checking our equipment and fleshing out our plans – was very much a proactive effort. We needed to slow down the pace of our work to ensure due diligence: nobody wanted to injure or kill another person by rushing through the eventual rescue, or through forgetting to check a vital piece of kit. (Which then might fail at the worst possible time.) In that moment, patience and care were essential traits.

And so much had already gone wrong! We had had to rescue workers trapped inside the cave. Saman had died while operating underwater. Those mysterious 'epileptic fits' too. But the most telling example of how moving too quickly could cause problems in a crisis situation was evidenced by those Thai Navy SEALs stuck in the cave alongside the Wild Boars. Had the military not been so determined to charge in, a plan might have been executed in such a way that all four operators could have swum back to the cave entrance without any drama. Instead, their eagerness to push the mission forward created an even bigger problem.

Rushing or panicking in a crisis is something that every one of us is guilty of from time to time. For some people it happens in a moment of high emotion. They hear something that upsets them in a domestic or business disagreement, and rather than slowing down and listening to the words that are actually being spoken, they crash headlong into a defensive position, which then only intensifies the conflict. Other people are guilty of agreeing to an exciting or potentially rewarding work commitment too quickly, only to discover a few days later that they have double-booked themselves, or over committed. The cancellation process can be embarrassing, but by simply stopping to think about what was being proposed in the first place, they could have saved a whole lot of grief.

Instead, in moments when immediate action is not required, it is often best to actively *do nothing*, and it's an option I have relied upon a lot while cave diving, especially if an exploration has become a little hairy. At times, when swimming into a new chamber for example, it's very common for the world around a diver to darken. A thick, cloudy sediment – puffed up by their movements – billows about them divers and during those dark moments, cocooned in the murk, the simple process of establishing up from down can seem difficult. It's not unusual to feel nauseous or dizzy when the senses have been cut off from any point of reference. Unaware of where they're going, a diver can panic. They might lose their grip on the line, or bump into a rocky outcrop or wall. But an experienced individual knows that if they are able to wait calmly for just a little while – in essence, *do nothing* – the sediment washing around them will eventually settle, and their visibility and bearings will return. They can then work their way forward.

The questions everybody should ask before reacting quickly in a crisis situation are these:

1) Will my immediate reactions make things worse?

2) Or will they move me towards where I want to be?

So in diving terms, does thrashing around in the water, desperately looking for a guideline, increase an individual's chance of survival in a risky situation? *No, they'll only become more confused and increasingly distanced from the correct way forward.* Does a bickering husband, or wife benefit from always charging headlong into a passionate defence of their actions during an argument? *Not likely, they'll only inflame the dispute and leave the other person feeling frustrated and misunderstood. They should instead listen and acknowledge the words of their partner.* In a lot of crisis situations, it is often far better to simply step back and read the events swirling around, rather than worsen the situation with a poorly considered word or action.

This is a theory I had previously stress-tested during a dive into Font del Truffe – a popular flooded cave in the Lot region of France. The appeal of exploring it was obvious: Font del Truffe's water was almost always crystal clear; a scenic, but small lake provided easy access to the spectacular underwater passages beyond, via one small squeeze down a gravel bank and under an arch. Once inside, the cave consisted of fourteen flooded sections, though most divers only visited the first couple of sumps. Rarely did anyone move beyond the fourth chamber because the effort to arrive there required a complex and heavy-going trudge through a dry cave while carrying lots of bulky equipment. At the very end, in the twelfth flooded section, an intimidating squeeze known as a rift had curtailed any previous explorations.

In the same way that mountaineering expeditions are planned in different ways, so it was possible to tackle Font del Truffe in one of two varied styles. The first was to move in the expedition manner, whereby a support team helped the lead divers by load-carrying any equipment over the tunnels' dry sections. The second method was to travel light and quickly, and with limited equipment. In the mountaineering world this was known as moving *alpine-style*, and Rick and I had chosen to follow this particular model. Our aim: to swim through the twelfth chamber, into the rift and then beyond.

Further strain was caused by the logistics of what promised to be a very tricky dive. In order to streamline ourselves, we decided to remove our buoyancy devices at the start of sump twelve so as to be able to squeeze through the final rift. Neither of us wanted to get our body pinned that deep inside Font del Truffe, but this only added to the complications we could expect at depth: without our buoyancy devices, there was every chance we might become *negatively buoyant*, meaning we'd be heavy enough to almost 'bottom walk' across the cave floor. Elsewhere, to ensure that we weren't overloaded with kit throughout the journey, we both staged various cylinders and equipment along the route. That way, we could collect and drop them off as we saw necessary, changing, or adjusting our essentials while progressing in a streamlined fashion. Every piece was vital. Missing just one changeover would scupper the trip; at worst it might prove fatal.

After negotiating over 2 kilometres (1.25 miles) of diving, interspersed with crawling, walking and some desperate climbs both up and down, we surfaced into the pool before sump twelve. As I looked at the desolate high rift ahead of me, the sheer smooth walls rose up from the water and stretched vertically into the blackness as far as my lights would penetrate. I realised there was no place here to exit the water even if I wanted to. I fastened my buoyancy devices to the guideline and recalled the plan. Rick was diving into the rift first; I would wait for ten minutes and then follow. And when my moment arrived, I swam down through a complex set of right-angled fissures in the rock, diving ever deeper, twisting and turning my way into the narrow passages. My view was incredible. The rock was spectacularly white, the water exceptionally clear, and ahead I noticed several wispy, granular curlicues – spirals of silt wafted up by Rick's fins as he had pressed ahead.

The cave's depth increased until, eventually I arrived at the previous limit of exploration – the deepest part of the sump. The visibility around me had worsened and, taking a moment to assess my location, I noticed the silt on the floor. There was plenty of it and a series of marks revealed where Rick had almost crawled along the bottom, laying a yellow guideline as he advanced. It disappeared into the inky blackness ahead – *the unknown*.

I shivered. The depths had compressed my wetsuit so tightly that the material seemed plastered to my body – it felt almost paper-thin and the cold pinched at my flesh. My nerves tingled too. And having followed Rick's line, I suddenly understood why previous divers had experienced second thoughts about progressing. The passage ahead resembled a living room fireplace and I'd have to crawl in and then up, into a stone tube that was no more than 50 centimetres (20 inches) wide. That would have been unsettling enough for anyone suffering from the slightest tremors of claustrophobia. However, I was at a depth of 30 metres (100 feet), a place where every sense became intensified. My head felt woozy from the narcosis of breathing from a rebreather, too, and given I was several kilometres from the surface, this was no place to get stuck. I would die, trapping Rick in the tunnels ahead – unless he was able to shift my corpse on the way out.

Taking a moment to settle I recalled a practised mantra for situations such as this: *I'm psychologically ready. I can do it. Stay calm.* Then I turned off my rebreather, hanging it parallel to my side in a line, so as to minimise my body profile. *In, out. In, out.* I felt my breath rising and falling through the regulator connected to my bailout cylinder*. At this depth I knew I had around a minute to spare, but beyond that, I risked using up too much gas and I would need every litre of it to exit Font del Truffe safely. My heart pounded as I wriggled into the submerged chimney.

Here we go.

The clock was ticking; this was no place to hang about, and I was forced to tackle the squeeze like a Victorian chimney sweep. Bending backwards unnaturally, I was able to wriggle inside, but only just, and without my buoyancy device I felt desperately heavy. Each pull and lift took me a little higher into the narrow channel. Every advance brought relief. My wetsuit was loosening as the water pressure released its grip, and slowly I became more buoyant. I started to float upwards until, at 20 metres (65 feet), the rift widened enough for me to swing my rebreather onto my chest. I could draw on my regular gas supply once more. Edging my way out of the shoulder-width tube and into an air space, I found Rick, beaming at me. We had extended the known limits of Font del Truffe.

And then the trouble began.

It was now my turn to lead, and having set our guideline through a beautiful, clean-washed passage to reach another air space, we had decided to turn around. Getting back would require us to negotiate the chimney once more, though at least this time we could allow gravity to do its work. Shifting my rebreather to one side, I plunged down the chute like a stone.

---

* Bailout cylinders are normally used when a diver's primary breathing apparatus fails, which in this case was the rebreather. In Font del Truffe we had decided to use our bailout cylinders on the way into the chimney to become as streamlined as possible, but this was considered unorthodox because doing so used up precious gas normally reserved for an emergency exit.

Having landed, the visibility at the bottom of the fireplace had dropped to zero thanks to my movements. Sediment now washed around me. I pushed off carefully, following the line by touch alone to surface in the air chamber on the safe side of sump twelve, where I could gather my kit.

Given we had repeated the same process for our entry into the further reaches of Font del Truffe, Rick should have been ten minutes behind me. *But he wasn't.* Ten minutes passed; then another twenty. Still there was no sign. I began to worry. And as more time ticked by, the moment had come to consider looking for Rick – *maybe he was stuck in the chimney, or worse?*

I realised that despite the brutal cold, there was no sense in rushing at that point. If Rick was underwater, I probably couldn't help him anyway. If he had been holding out in an air space, he would be fairly safe. It made sense to wait and let the water clear. The alternative was to rush into a search that might have been either pointless or counter-productive – I could have wasted valuable gas or become trapped while looking for someone who either did not need urgent help, or was dead. (In which case, he was beyond helping.) Blundering around in the murk wasn't going to do anyone any favours. Up to my neck in the water, I hung around and shivered. I had taken the *do nothing* option.

After about an hour, and with still no sign of Rick, I contemplated swimming back through the sump. I knew the murky water would have cleared a little by then, though it would still be churning with silt. I would have waited longer, but I had the sneaking suspicion that hanging about for too long might prove costly – I had felt the first tell-tale signs of oncoming hypothermia, which wasn't surprising given I'd been floating in the icy cold for so long. Getting warm would soon be my next priority. Then suddenly, a glimmer above caught my eye. *It was a set of lights*. They were attached to a red helmet and it was moving about in the dry section of the cave above. From the same direction, a familiar voice yelled at me.

'What are you doing down there?'

Bloody hell, it was Rick! Apparently, he had followed me underwater, down the chimney and into the murk at the bottom of the fireplace. At that point, he had come across a loose end of frayed line rather than the guideline that would have led him to safety. Disorientated, he then composed himself for a few moments in the dark, before making a brief attempt at finding the rift that would lead him out. Stranded in murky waters, and realising the task was impossible, he retreated back up the chimney and into to the last airspace we'd found. Once there, he waited for the sediment to settle.

Handily for him, he had been able to wait it out on dry ground, where he relaxed on a small clump of boulders while I shivered, neck-deep in the water. Never one to miss an opportunity, he then went exploring and discovered a dry bypass over the top of sump twelve – it's from there that he had spotted me. To this day though, Rick still maintains I cut the line in order to trap him inside Font del Truffe forever, a theory he obviously hadn't thought through in any real forensic detail: there's no way I'd have stumped up the entire fuel costs for my return trip back to the UK. I needed his wallet.

But our episode in France clearly illustrated the power of the *do nothing* option. Rick and I had found ourselves on very different, but equally precarious, sides of the same incident. And independently of one another we had both arrived at the same conclusion. Don't make things worse. *Let the silt settle*. Our patience and calm thinking in the early stages of a crisis situation resulted in a swift and satisfactory resolution. Had Rick used up too much gas by searching for the exit at depth, there is a chance he might not have made it out at all. Had I bolted for the surface to raise the alarm unnecessarily, I'd have been forced to attempt a risky solo exit and Rick could have been stuck inside until help arrived. Handily, the outcome was very different. We made it out alive.

HURRY UP AND DO . . . *NOTHING*: THE CHECKLIST

- Allow volatile situations to settle. Don't stir the silt.
- Take action only if it moves you towards your goal. Otherwise, pause.
- Embrace uncertainty. Remember, the zero-risk option doesn't exist.

LESSON #10

KEEP IT SIMPLE

The greatest plans are those that are underpinned by a devilish simplicity, whose architects have a keen understanding of the minimum level of complexity required to succeed. But all too often, our processes become needlessly overcomplicated, factoring in a myriad of 'What if's?' – many of which might never occur in reality. I've learned that an excessively cautious approach tends to create systems, or processes, with so many options, branches and safeguards that their parts begin to interact in a way the designers never foresaw. Frustratingly, these defences can cause more issues than the very events they were intended to solve.

When planning any project, it's necessary to strike a balance in which the scheme remains as uncomplicated as possible while ensuring that any predictable problems or catastrophes can still be dealt with effectively. In Tham Luang, we were ready to walk that very tightrope. Balance would be everything . . .

DAY ELEVEN
THURSDAY 6 JULY 2018

So what was the plan?

Given how protracted the rescue operation needed to be, and how its success would hinge on organisation and logistics, Rick took the unusual step of going back to the drawing board – quite literally. A survey of the cave was obtained, and a map sketched on to an A2 board that morning. Detailing every air chamber and cavern, plus dive base and the line locations – and, of course, the gloomy space in which the Wild Boars had been pinned – the map was then overlaid with several sheets of clear plastic. Each one allowed us to add and remove relevant features, such as any potential spots where we could stage air cylinders, or areas in which to swap our equipment. By studying the map, everyone was able to visualise the terrain ahead of us more accurately.

I can remember how Rick's board was initially viewed in some quarters with scepticism. Certainly, the idea of his taking an entire morning to draw out a map appeared to be an unaffordable extravagance. But once the schematics of Tham Luang were relocated to the US Air Force encampment, our A2 map became a vital cog in the rescue machine: it was referred to continually throughout planning meetings and briefings, but more than anything, it served as a reminder of just how complicated the Wild Boars' extraction would be. And so we worked hard to ensure our processes remained as uncomplicated as possible. If ever the phrase '*Keep it simple*' seemed appropriate, it was during those discussions as Rick and I worked with the American military to establish an uncomplicated, but *realistic* plan. There was no point in rushing, either. We were in Thailand for the long haul.

Eventually our planning focused on four key areas:

1. The extraction process.
2. Equipment.
3. The team.
4. The transportation of the boys as we swam them through the caves.

I'll run through them in detail. . .

1) THE EXTRACTION PROCESS

All manner of imaginative suggestions were being sent our way from the public. Some were delivered to us directly, others arrived via the British Cave Rescue Council. The senders had been tuned into our predicament thanks, in part, to the twenty-four hour news cycle in place, but very few of the notes were helpful. In the outside world, everybody had suddenly become an armchair guru on the subject of cave rescues, and the tone underpinning 99.9 per cent of what could only be described as brain farts was one of assumed expertise: 'Children's lives are at stake. I can save them! *You have to listen to me.*' Having said that, a few caught my eye, mainly because they were so outlandish.

#1: The Great Sausage Plan
The scheme: *'Why don't you run a one-metre- diameter plastic tube from your dive base to the children? You could inflate it somehow and then have them all crawl to safety?'*

Reality check: The Great Sausage Plan would have required around 1.5 kilometres (1 mile) of highly durable plastic in order to work. Even if the tube *could* have been laid through Tham Luang (spoiler alert: it couldn't), any leak that sprung as the children moved inside would have been disastrous. The tube would have collapsed, trapping everybody in much the same way a skin, or membrane, binds the sausage meat in a pork banger. (Hence the name, The Great Sausage Plan.)

#2: Drill For Victory!

The scheme: *'Here's an idea: why don't you drill a hole from the top of the mountain all the way down to where the children are sheltering? Then you can winch them out.'*

Reality check: The speleological survey covering the Tham Luang system wasn't anywhere near accurate enough, so locating those kids from a kilometre (over half a mile) above would have been close to impossible. Also, who knew what the geological implications of such an effort might be? Sure, this style of rescue had previously worked when thirty-three workers became trapped inside a Chilean mine in 2010, but that was only possible because the area and the tunnels had been surveyed in much greater detail.

#3: The Yellow Submarine Plan

The scheme: *'Why don't you use Gamow bags (an inflatable, hyperbaric bag used to treat people when suffering from altitude sickness) to transport the kids? You can seal them inside, one by one, and move them through the tunnel.'*

Reality check: Like The Great Sausage Plan, one tear would result in the single sausage collapsing and leaking, drowning the boy inside. And that's if the tubes were able to fit around the bends in the passage, which they wouldn't. (There was also the 1,000 kilos (2,200 pounds) of weight required to sink the thing.)

#4 Swim For Your Life!

The Scheme: 'Why don't you teach the children to become expert scuba divers, then have them make their first-ever cave dive downstream guided by two divers – one in front and one behind.'

Reality Check: We had been told that many of the Wild Boars couldn't actually swim, and none of them had any diving experience. We had already been given a reminder of just how difficult this process would be a couple of days previously, having dragged those Thai water-workers through three short sumps. (Saman, a former Thai Navy SEAL, had also died.) Even with underwater support, at some point the children would inevitably panic and drown themselves – and probably their rescuers – due to a lack of communication and experience.

#5: The SpongeBob SquarePants Plan

The Scheme: *'Couldn't you use a series of giant sponges to soak up the water and then transport them away?'*

Reality check: I think the flaws in this one are fairly obvious, don't you?

These suggestions, while well meaning, ended up being nothing more than an occasional moment of light relief from the stressful atmosphere that was building around us – a mixture of fatigue, anxiety and tension. Rick and I knew that to succeed we would have to think in an entirely different way to everyone else, by stripping back the very concept of a rescue to its barest bones and eliminating as many complications as possible. What resulted was a scheme that appeared incredibly basic in theory: *One diver takes one child and transports him throughout the entire flooded section of the cave, while the passenger breathes through a single demand valve* all the way.* But there was a caveat to this idea that betrayed its undeniable fragility: *There would be very little redundancy of equipment and, therefore, zero room to screw up.* While there were clearly a number of risks in play because, well, cave diving is inherently full of risks, it really was the best option on the table.

2) EQUIPMENT

The equipment required for moving the boys through the cave in such a way needed to be user-friendly (for us) and incredibly safe (for them). We decided that the most logical approach would be to treat each kid like the type of objects that were transited during a typical exploration dive. Luckily for us, we had only to think about transporting the children through the flooded sumps because once we reached dive base they would be handed to another team, such as the Thai military, who would be far better suited to carrying them over the dryer sections of the cavern near the entrance. The Navy SEALs trapped in chamber nine would also act as translators both to explain the plan to the Wild Boars, and to help to provide instructions. Having decided that we would manoeuvre the kids as though they were air

---

* Open-circuit breathing apparatus usually come in two parts. The first connects to the cylinder and reduces the pressure within to a level that can be inhaled and exhaled. The second – the demand valve – is held in the diver's mouth and triggers the air flow whenever he, or she inhales.

cylinders, or habitats, the idea then gathered a codename: *The Package Plan*.

Our equipment was tested and retested to the nth degree because there would be zero redundancy on the air supply feeding into the children's masks. That meant if a demand valve, or its first-stage regulator were to fail, the child relying upon it would likely not survive. To address this problem we serviced and then thoroughly tested these critical pieces of equipment daily, before each and every use. Meanwhile, we decided to dress each boy in a 'horse collar' buoyancy compensator, the kind that was used by the Thai Navy, and were in plentiful supply. Leg loops and elastic attachments were added to hold the oxygen cylinders; extra control was created by ensuring that the jacket would fit each boy snugly and couldn't move around; and we decided to tie ourselves to the children in transit with a lanyard. That way, if one of us had to release a boy during an emergency situation, he wouldn't drift away in the murk.

Modifications of this kind were very much in our territory – Rick and I had long tailored our equipment to suit the explorations we undertook. Meanwhile, British divers were well known for making what were nicknamed 'bottle bras' from elastic loops and pieces of inner tubes that were designed to hold one or two cylinders loosely on the chest. We were comfortable when thinking outside of the box, though every change or adaptation was made with simplicity in mind. Inventing a complicated new apparatus in the limited time available to us in Thailand was out of the question. While we needed to be imaginative, we couldn't be *too* imaginative – it would only cause problems further down the line.

Meanwhile, the American Air Force, having understood the simple elegance of what we were hoping to achieve, worked to mass-produce our prototype buoyancy jacket. By the end of the day, just about every hardware store in Chiang Rai had been bought out of elastic bungee cord. When those supplies were eventually exhausted, the local stock of elastic roof-rack straps were snapped up too. (Bad news for anyone hoping to fix something to the car that week.) Meanwhile, child-sized wetsuits had arrived from all over the country, though the majority of them appeared to be on the larger side. Knowing there was inevitably going to be some element of making-do, we hung on to the smallest ones and hoped for the best.

When it came to preparing the kids' masks for the rescue mission, however, nobody was willing to accept anything other than perfection. A large number of full-face masks were shipped in from all over the world, and each one covered the eyes, nose, mouth and chin with a clear plastic screen, sealed with a rubber skirt, and were secured by a spider's web of straps that wrapped around the back of the head, much like a fireman's mask, but watertight. Unfortunately, many of them just weren't suitable, for one reason or another. We decided that the kids should wear constant positive air pressure masks, a piece of kit that ensured the air pressure inside was set slightly above the ambient pressure in the water. The mask was important for a reason: the pressure inside it would help push more gas into the lungs of the boys, and this, coupled with the oxygen-rich mixture we were using would give them the best possible chance of survival.

For much of the time, the media looked in on our work through long lenses with bemusement. They were unused to the idea that a rescue could be held together with nylon tape, large rubber bands and bungee cords, *A-Team*-style, but that's how

Rick and I liked to operate. Our armoury of tools was slowly coming together.

3) THE TEAM

Now we needed to decide which of the divers within the rescue teams were best suited to what had been planned. When discussing our options, I could really only think of four lead divers to swim the boys out – Rick and myself, plus Jason and Chris. The inclusion of the Euro Team as support divers and Connor, Josh and Jim, together with our Australian colleagues would ultimately prove key. For *The Package Plan* to function, a series of dumps, or caches, needed to be established in certain chambers so that the lead divers could swap kit and switch air cylinders. Claus and Mikko would provide invaluable assistance during those changeovers. They would also help the carry the boys over the rocky stretches between sumps.

Before long, our entire plan, right down to the final detail, had been laid out on the A2 board. We understood the granular points of cylinder strategy and our sequence of extraction; we knew how the kids would be dressed, and that they would use a rich oxygen mix in their cylinders. The idea was that their blood would become saturated with as much oxygen as possible. That would increase their chances of survival slightly, should their supply unexpectedly fail, though that also depended on us reaching an air space to resuscitate them successfully. In the end, an 80 per cent mixture was all that was available to us. It definitely wasn't ideal.

The individuals working on the ground had details to learn,

too. For example, most people were probably familiar with the idea that casualties are usually positioned face-up when being transported on a stretcher. And while this technique works perfectly well in an above-ground environment, in an underwater cave rescue it could lead to a fatality. *Why?* Well, when wearing a full-face mask, of the type we were using, the face-up casualty could potentially choke and drown on any water that had pooled inside. When lying face down, however, that same water would gather harmlessly around the screen of the mask rather than about the mouth and nose. We made a note reminding everyone that the kids should be transported *face-down*, especially when underwater.

To counter this problem further, we added lead weights to a pocket in the front of their buoyancy jackets and planned to attach a heavy cylinder to the chest. Both modifications would act as a keel, holding the wearer face down and in a stable, horizontal position —a bit like a boat – so that a safe position could be maintained in the water as they were dragged along. We could also 'park' the boys on the cave floor if necessary, confident that their face mask and diving regulator would remain clear of the mud. Given we only had four lead divers – Rick, Jason, Chris and myself – we would only be able to retrieve four boys a day. This matched up nicely with the fact that we'd only been able to source four reliable masks.

4) TRANSPORTING THE WILD BOARS

There was one thorny issue we hadn't yet addressed: *how the hell were we going to stop the boys from panicking or thrashing about underwater?*

Then Rick made a dark suggestion. 'Let's carry the kids out unconscious,' he said.

At first I thought I had misheard him. By the looks of it, so did the others in the room. Everyone gawped.

What do you mean?

'Maybe we should sedate them?'

While this might have sounded incredibly cold, it did deal with one of the most pressing complications within *The Package Plan*, which was that unlike air cylinders, or habitats, the packages in question would not in any way be inert. They were young boys; they would be frightened. Some of them would freak out, wriggle and potentially die while being dragged through the murky waters, spaces that had intimidated plenty of experienced divers working on the operation. (These meltdowns might also put the rescuers at risk.) But by using sedation, the logistical problems of moving the boys would be translated into a medical issue, one that appeared much simpler to solve – we only had to find someone who could figure out a suitable drug and dosage. The idea was kicked up the chain of command for consideration.

While we awaited their response, Rick's sedation theory was floated with Doctor Richard 'Harry' Harris – a professional aeromedical consultant and an anaesthetist with the South Australian Ambulance Service. Harry was also an experienced cave diver, and had been at home, packing for an expedition to the Nullarbor cave region on the southern coast of Australia when we contacted him. The response to Rick's texted message was emphatic.

NO. ABSOLUTELY NOT.

Harry sensibly pointed out that the use of anaesthetics still presented certain risks, even in an operating theatre surrounded by the paraphernalia of modern medical equipment and support personnel. He then went on to explain the medical concerns regarding the sedation of malnourished and dehydrated kids stuck inside a cave. But we were all out of other options. Rick was determined to press the issue.

'If we do nothing, they're all going to die,' he said.

Eventually, Harry agreed to be persuaded and then, if the evidence proved compelling enough, he would reconsider.

'I'll come to Thailand to assess the situation myself,' he said. 'And I'll bring my dive partner, Craig Challen, too.'

Craig was an experienced diver and a full-time vet, and with no time to lose, the logistical details of what would be required should Harry give us the thumbs-up were thrashed out between Rick and myself. Both of us reckoned on Harry siding with the plan, especially once he had seen the Wild Boars' predicament close up, and so the mission was renamed as *The Inert Package Plan*. But none of us had really thought out the realities of such a sedation event. Not fully, anyway. When first imagining the process, I had pictured a woozy kid with floppy limbs. He was able to hold eye contact and carried just enough presence of mind to respond to my commands. I soon learned that this had been an oversight on my part, and I would have to revise my visualisation of exactly what was coming down the line, as well as the details regarding the kids' physical state during the rescue. The truth, when it arrived, would seem very unnerving.

Ketamine was discussed as the sedative of choice, and for good reason: it would render the boys completely unconscious and that ensured they would have no memory of their traumatic journey. Most important of all was the effect it had on a person's breathing. A number of studies had been conducted by the

Australian Antarctic Survey, in which a group of seals had been administered ketamine. The results had shown that the mammals airways remained fully functional despite having fallen unconscious. It was hoped that this characteristic, combined with the positive pressure masks, would ensure the Wild Boars' breathing remained stable throughout their extraction. That's not to say we felt 100 per cent comfortable with the decision. Sedating Antarctic seals was one thing. Sedating humans and then swimming them underwater for 1.5 kilometres (1 mile) and carrying them over rocky stretches represented a desperate rescue effort, and had never been attempted before.

■ ■ ■

All of us understood that *The Inert Package Plan* was risky. Certain of its factors felt familiar, such as the terrain in the cave and the changeovers of air cylinders. Others were terrifyingly unique – I had never rescued a kid before, let alone a heavily sedated one, and I was reminded of a phrase once used by the American Secretary for Defence, Donald Rumsfeld during his slightly unusual statement in 2002 regarding the Iraqi government led by Saddam Hussein.

'Reports that say that something hasn't happened are always interesting to me, because as we know, there are known knowns; there are things we know we know. We also know there are known unknowns; that is to say we know there are some things we do not know. But there are also unknown unknowns – the ones we don't know we don't know. And if one looks throughout the history of our country and other free countries, it is the latter category that tends to be the difficult ones.'

Rumsfeld was mocked for this statement, but the thought

processes behind it seemed relevant to our situation in Tham Luang. In our case, the *known knowns* represented the cave and the kids; the route, our plan and the equipment at our disposal. Those spinning plates we could handle. The *unknown unknowns* were events that we really couldn't plan for because they were unseen problems, or disasters that might emerge from left field. For those, I would have to rely upon our experience, flexible thinking, or the Library of Plans. But it was the *known unknowns* that unsettled me the most – the worst-case scenario.

What if a child died as I tried to manoeuvre him through Tham Luang?

The thought had certainly crossed my mind. When considering the possibility of sedation, it was hard not to feel vulnerable, and I understood that the repercussions would be incredibly painful, not just for the child's family, but for me as well. If the worst-case scenario unfolded, there might even be legal issues to consider, too. And my unease was only increased by the news that Harry Harris and Craig Challen were being granted diplomatic immunity for their work in Thailand. That meant if one of the Wild Boars died while under their supervision, the Australians would be able to leave without charge.

We had been offered no such luxury.

The threat of imprisonment was something I needed to set aside for now. My focus had to be on moving the boys safely through the cave. I reassured myself that the team had experience of transiting unusual, unwieldy objects through fast-moving water during all sorts of explorations. A dry tube, or diving habitat were equally challenging loads, and shifting them had provided experience and understanding for the graft ahead. The difference was that, despite their comparable bulk and weight, those items weren't as valuable or as precious as a human life. That truth would prove to be the biggest psychological test of all.

SIMPLE AND RELIABLE DELIVERS SUCCESS

Simplicity is key when planning for success, as so many self-development and business books tell us, but reliability is also an incredibly important factor, even though it can add complexity. I've found that striking a balance between the two is vital. For example, when working on getting the kids out of Tham Luang, the *most reliable* solution would have involved adding a higher number of divers and diving cylinders to the Inert Package Plan. This would have improved our ability to change equipment underwater in the event of a failure, but it would have also added significant complexity, to the point where an accident or error was almost inevitable.

Instead, we chose the *simplest* solution on the table and then figured out how we could make the process as reliable as possible. In the dangerous environment of Tham Luang, we used the bare minimum of equipment and personnel. But what we sacrificed in complex reliability, we more than made up for with our experience, training and equipment.

By trying to make a process too safe, or too foolproof, by adding layers of complexity, a system can actually become less reliable and maybe even destined for failure. A good example of this is the human daisy chain concept as a suggestion to rescue the children. On paper, having more personnel in the water should have been a significant advantage, but Rick and I sensed there were just too many moving parts involved to succeed. For example, communication issues between the divers would only increase the potential for human error. The idea was so complicated as to be actually dangerous.

I have found the best way to deliver the most *suitable* levels of reliability is to consider: 1) the environment in which the system must operate; 2) the outcome required; and 3) the appropriate cost for that outcome. So, in Tham Luang, our objective was to save as many kids as possible without unnecessarily compromising the safety of the rescuers involved. With that objective established and keeping the diving conditions in mind – we then devised a system we knew would work safely and carried the minimal amount of excess baggage. We traded off complexity and redundancy for a simple system that was appropriate given the low visibility and poor conditions in the cave.

When cave diving, my objectives have always been well defined: I wanted to explore caves or rescue other cavers and not die in the process. Selecting equipment to achieve these objectives isn't always easy, though, and occasionally I have struck the wrong balance. One occasion when this was brought into sharp relief was during an exploration dive into Wookey Hole in 2005, a year on from our successful exploration where we'd been able to extend the cave beyond Rob Parker's recorded limit. I remember we could have gone further in 2004. Despite discovering an ascending, open passage beyond the bottom of the sump – some 76 metres (250 feet) down – we turned around, even though we sensed it might lead us towards an undiscovered surface. Sadly, I was at the limit of my bailout gas; the decompression penalty*

---

* Decompression penalty is the amount of time a diver must remain underwater decompressing, ascending only slowly to avoid the bends.

was too great. Having been disappointed, my aim when I returned in 2005 was to find a technical solution to this problem.

I planned all winter. Accompanied by a team of divers from the self-styled National Union of Rebreather Porters, which included team leader, Duncan Price, we carried a large number of cylinders into Wookey Hole. (The group name was a light-hearted reference; the porters in question were paid in beer.) I decided that even with additional safety cylinders, a single rebreather wouldn't be sufficient for such an exploration and so I doubled up, attaching rebreathers to my side and chest. Another small air cylinder was added to inflate my drysuit, as well as a second oxygen cylinder for my additional rebreather. (Oh, and two side-mounted cylinders I'd used the previous year. *Did I mention I might have got the balance wrong?*) I also decided to take a hand-held light with a battery pack, which I then strapped to a cylinder. Having managed a handful of practice dives with the new setup, I felt relatively confident it would prove successful, but I had overcomplicated my situation dramatically.

I had become unreliable.

Between us, Rick and I had a clear plan of what we wanted to happen inside the cave. Due to the complexity of the dive, we had agreed that we should take turns at leading the exploration. Technically, we would be diving alone, but we figured it was sensible to assist one another by placing emergency cylinders at the decompression zone for the returning explorer. We had reckoned that in the event of an incident, the spare gas in place would be sufficient for one person, and it would prove so much better than sharing, as we had done a year previously. (Though the dives would now be longer and more complex.) For the first trip, Rick was set to support me, but as he swam into the darkness,

I experienced a disconcerting flush of loneliness, and a creeping feeling of discomfort as I readied my kit – *I was too bulky*. On previous dives into Wookey Hole I had travelled lightly, and had felt comfortable. *But now?* Well now something was off. My inner voice was whispering. 'It'll be all right,' but at that stage in my life I hadn't figured out how to listen. Foolishly, I submerged and kicked off into the depths.

The claustrophobic sensation of carrying too much gear, *of overcomplicating things*, instantly felt smothering. With so much equipment wrapped around me, I didn't feel streamlined enough; the umbilical cord of my hand-held light snagged on the walls and rocky outcrops as I swam. This should have been a warning sign. Instead, I pressed on regardless, emboldened by the sediment trails in the water ahead, evidence that Rick was making good progress. Having reached the first squeeze at a depth of 65 metres (215 feet) – a narrow chute of gravel and darkness about the width of a British postbox – I readied myself for the nerve-wracking wriggle inside.

Trouble landed almost immediately. The tight section was only 5 metres (15 feet) long, but the passage sloped down at an awkward angle of around 25 degrees. Stony nodules pockmarked the ceiling and I recalled from previous dives that to crawl through I would have to remove my rebreather and push it in front of me. (Though to make progress I'd still need to plough a body-wide furrow in the gravel floor ahead.) It was around this time that the issues with my overcomplicated setup presented themselves in full.

I had been navigating a zig-zagging course by moving around the bumps in the ceiling, while searching to locate every inch of space ahead, when, without warning ... *everything became jammed*. I was stuck fast. I felt around and realised my equipment had wedged me tight. The smaller cylinders I had so carefully positioned around my body on the surface had moved from their designated places were being gripped by the rock around me; my hands were restricted by the cord of the flashlight and everything was entangled. Worse, a small gravel shelf had gathered in front of my chest and was blocking any forward movement. I would have to back out – if it were even possible. A smothering, bear hug of panic enfolded me.

The funny thing about side-mounted cylinders is that they are fairly inconspicuous when moving forward. They attach to the waist, held in place at their necks by a loop of elastic, and the cylinders tuck neatly under a diver's arms in a streamlined fashion as they swim forward. Annoyingly, this aerodynamic arrangement tends to collapse when moving in reverse. The cylinders splay out, acting like the barb on a fishhook. Rebreathers and attachments spread out like an enraged octopus as all manner of webbing and equipment react to the reversed movement – my escape had been made doubly difficult because I was attempting to wriggle out feet first uphill and escaping from the squeeze's pincer-like grip seemed impossible. And then I noticed Rick. He was a little ahead of me, just beyond the chute and filming my desperate movements. As far as he was concerned, my predicament was going to make for some great viewing later on. What he hadn't realised was quite how stuck I was, or that he would also be trapped if I couldn't figure out some method of escape.

Unable to move, I took the only option available to me: I reached around to detach the equipment fixing me in place. Fastenings were unclipped; cylinders were removed; until, thankfully, after what felt like hours – though it was probably only fifteen minutes or so – I had become streamlined enough to move. Unable to reverse, I pushed at the gravel ahead and forced a route down and out of the squeeze. After some effort I landed on the wrong side of the obstacle in a tangle of disconnected equipment. I was frustrated. Given I had struggled so much in negotiating the first squeeze, it was clear that the second would be beyond me, too. I also had used up about as much composure as I had to spare that day. I signalled to Rick that I was turning round and made my way back, decompressing as I swam to the surface. I had wasted both my turn at exploration and the time and efforts of the National Union of Rebreather Porters.

Wookey Hole has long been considered an area of historical significance in the cave-diving community. Generations of explorers have made their mark inside, especially as new technologies were developed and pioneered: bottom-walking* divers first went there during the 1930s and walked along the rocky floor; the initial use of scuba air tanks by early frogmen happened at Wookey Hole; in the 1980s the first successful use of helium-based diving mixes in caves took place. I had previously been fortunate enough to make my mark there by using modern rebreathers for the first time, plus a newly developed dive computer called the VR3. By attempting to push the known limits of Wookey Hole with Rick that day, I had hoped extend the cave once more. Thanks to my overcomplicated plan, I had failed. Worse, on our next dive inside, it would be my turn to take the supporting role.

---

* Bottom walking is a method of propulsion where divers wear lead boots and literally walk along the floor underwater. It is associated with commercial diving or very early diving systems.

But Rick had other ideas. 'I guess it's still your turn the next time,' he said as we packed our kit away later that day.

Really? I'd never known Rick to hand over a lead before – or since, for that matter.

'Yeah, your turn didn't really count. And if you can come up with a simpler plan than the one you had today, it'll be fine.'

But I was way ahead of him; my lesson had been learned. Striking the balance between simplicity and reliability, I realised, would be key if I were to succeed. And as I'd fumed through my decompression a few hours previously, it had become apparent that the less-is-more approach was going to be more appropriate for a challenge of this kind. Stripping back my equipment in order to wriggle more easily through the first squeeze would be a good start. And when we returned to Wookey Hole a fortnight later, I took the bare minimum of kit required for a two rebreather setup, and I successfully continued our exploration into the depths of the cave until a boulder choke blocked my path. Rick took another go a month later, and confirmed that we could go no further, though he had chosen to carry just the one rebreather. At the time, I had worried that by travelling so light, Rick's air supplies might prove dangerously limiting. This hunch was confirmed when he refused to show anyone his cylinder contents gauge after surfacing. When asked in an interview about just how much gas he'd had left in the tank, Rick shrugged.

'Enough,' he said. *'But not plenty.'*

KEEP IT SIMPLE: THE CHECKLIST

- Define your need for reliability. Don't overcomplicate the plan.

- Understand the cost of failure. Calculate the value of reliability.

- Choose the simplest possible solution. *Better* is the enemy of *Good enough*.

LESSON #11

REHEARSE. THEN REPEAT

Any number of challenges or demanding projects can benefit from a little preparation in the form of rehearsal and visualisation. The rehearsal part is the easy bit. For example, it's often helpful to run through how we want to present ourselves during a job interview, or to practise a stressful work briefing in front of friends, or a mirror.

Visualisation is really just another form of practice, but rather than physically rehearsing the issue ahead, we see it playing out in our minds. When cave diving, I've often imagined myself performing a set of procedures underwater, which has later helped me to execute the task successfully. I have also learned to apply two abstract techniques:

1. The visualisation of feelings, which requires me to imagine – and actually feel – the true effort and emotions might experience in order to achieve my goals.

2. The visualisation of disaster, where I picture and prepare myself for what could go wrong before reaching into the Library of Plans for a solution.

All of these methods were applied as we worked to extract the Wild Boars from Tham Luang. And with a little imagination, I've found they can be used in all manner of day-to-day situations, too . . .

DAY TWELVE
SATURDAY 7 JULY 2018

Drawing together all that strategy and procedure – not to mention our modified equipment – into a coherent plan was one thing. Putting that plan into action was a whole other matter entirely. With Harry and Craig now installed at Tham Luang, they were soon able to negotiate the sedation elements of *the Inert Package Plan*, but not before consulting with a list of medical experts to ensure we weren't crossing any ethical or procedural boundaries. Having received the go-ahead from a number of eminent Australian medics, the two divers then swam into chamber nine to meet with the Wild Boars. Harry's immediate response was a positive one. Because of the severe situation, he was agreeable to sedating the kids, though there was a caveat.

'But I won't be swimming them out,' he said.

Given the difficulty of the dive, I could see his point.

What followed appeared to be a game of political tennis in which our rescue plan, along with the thorny issue of sedation, was batted from one authority to the next. The consequences and optics of sticking a football team and their coach with syringes full of ketamine – which, let's not forget, had previously gathered some notoriety as a party drug – were potentially explosive. If anything went wrong, or someone died, the backlash was sure to be seismic. Despite the fact that both the parents and the boys had agreed to the plan, they couldn't fully comprehend the risks, and in many ways they had been caught between a rock and a hard place: if the kids were injected with a sedative and then moved underwater through the caves, there was a chance they might die in an accident. The alternative was to leave them stuck inside, a decision that would inevitably result in their deaths. I was pleased not to be privy to those conversations, and they continued for another day or so.

And then, after a number of phone calls and heated discussions, the authorities signed off on the proposal – in theory.

We were on.

Though the extraction process was yet to receive an official start time, we pressed ahead with our preparations. We planned a session of rescue rehearsals so we could gain a greater understanding of how the boys might move as they were transported through the churning waters of Tham Luang. The only problem was . . . *where?* Eventually, the local swimming pool was commandeered for us for a day. It had also been arranged that four boys, all of varying shapes and sizes – a short and tall kid; one skinny, one big – from a swimming club in Chiang Rai, would represent the various members of the Wild Boars. That would allow us to perform a full test of our positive pressure masks and modified buoyancy devices. Unsurprisingly, when our proposed session was announced, it was greeted with doubt in some quarters.

But then, everything we had attempted or announced so far had drawn attention – both inside the rescuing planning sessions and beyond. As we drove to the pool, Rick's phone began to beep. He looked at the screen.

'I think it's Elon Musk,' he said, sounding exasperated.

Amid the flurry of communications that were pouring in from all over the world, Musk's was probably the most high-profile of all. The Tesla CEO and chief designer at SpaceX had requested various logistical details – he had wanted to learn more about the dynamics of the cave and the nature of the passage inside. Rick was not that familiar with Musk's work; he had little interest in his reputation and achievements and seemed somewhat unimpressed. But I was aware of his accomplishments. As someone with more than a passing interest in SpaceX's activities, I reckoned Musk was well positioned to offer a useful suggestion or two. Given the almost unlimited resources at his disposal, there was every chance he might come up with an idea or contribute some detail we hadn't yet considered.

'Look, I know we're getting crap like The Great Sausage Plan, but it would be foolish to refuse the help of someone like Elon Musk,' I said. 'He's asking us for information, and it won't take long to provide him with it. Why don't we just feed him what he's asking for and treat it as a wild card? I can't tell you if he's going to be useful, but if anyone can pull this off, *Iron Man*-style, he's as close an option as we're going to get.'

Rick answered the phone. His tone was a little grumpy.

'Hello, *Elon?*'

Group conversations around a mobile are complicated at the best of times – people tend to talk over one another; all sorts of miscommunications can occur, and it's not uncommon for someone to feel slighted, or ignored in the crossfire. When that conversation takes place in the back of a packed minibus, the atmosphere can feel incredibly awkward, especially as Rick had the phone pressed close to his ear. Elon spoke to Rick. I listened and interjected where I could. Rick relayed the message. A meeting of minds that carried the potential for some interesting forward movement, with maybe the germ of an idea or a resource that might have proved invaluable, quickly died on the vine. The noise in the minibus increased as the driver accelerated. Rick was struggling to hear. I watched as his focus drifted back to our work for the day.

'Well, look, I'm sorry, I have to go now,' he said, searching for the off button on his phone.

I was taken aback. *Did Rick really just hang up on Elon Musk?**

But Rick seemed untroubled. 'I've got things to do,' he said.

He had a point. It was already clear that the Thai authorities were taking very few chances with our rehearsal. When we eventually arrived at the swimming pool, the car park was jammed. At least four ambulances had been stationed outside and all of them had their doors open in anticipation of some terrible incident. And we hadn't yet pulled on our wetsuits. The uneasy sense that we weren't to be trusted with four young lives was amplified further once we stepped into the facility. A huge audience made up of local officials, military figures and civilian doctors and paramedics had gathered to watch the procedure. The mood was ghoulish, as if none of them expected us to succeed.

We were watched like hawks. Camera phones recorded our every move and it was suddenly hard not to anticipate the worst happening. Mindful of the consequences of an accident, I felt very envious of Harry's diplomatic immunity status as we managed the boys into our redesigned buoyancy devices and guided them to the pool's edge. As well as practising the extraction techniques required to save the Wild Boars, our

---

* I later learned that Musk was kindly offering to construct a submarine from rocket parts, and while his capsule eventually found its way to Tham Luang, it was never used. Sadly, his involvement didn't end there. Musk became embroiled in a court case with another British caver involved in the rescue. I'm glad to say I wasn't involved with that unwelcome distraction.

bedside manner was being put to the test too: through a translator we explained what was about to take place, before reassuring and cajoling our test subjects as we pulled them under the water. At certain points I asked that they try to keep as still as possible, and having suggested that any feeling of fear, or discomfort should be communicated by a squeeze of the hand, I soon realised there were actually more complications to consider during a rehearsal than there would be inside Tham Luang. For starters we were planning on sedating the Wild Boars, so they weren't likely to wriggle or thrash underwater. There also wouldn't be a viewing gallery of stony-faced spectators inside chamber nine.

Eventually, Rick, Jason, Chris and I went to work. And as the large crowd looked on nervously, our volunteers were transported this way and that, the handles attached to their backs holding firm. In the worst-case scenario drill, where I imagined losing hold of a kid, it was possible to relocate him by pulling the lanyard attached to the boy's harness. Elsewhere, the lead weight at the front of our 'casualty's' buoyancy device prevented him from rolling in the water. Our procedure had stood up to scrutiny, and when I eventually pulled away my face mask and looked around the swimming pool, the crowd was dispersing. The doom-laden vibe had passed. Even the gathered medics, all of them on tenterhooks at the start of the session, were now staring at their phones absentmindedly. By the looks of it, we had brought the authorities around to our line of thinking.

We were on to something.

Kidding myself into believing that the hard yards had been completed was a dangerous move, though. I recognised that the challenges ahead were still undeniably difficult, and dangerous, but there was reassurance in the fact that our instincts had been correct. *The Inert Package Plan* was feasible. After another hour or so underwater, we could see that both the British and Euro teams were very much up to the task. Any diver that might have felt uncertain or rusty when negotiating some of the finer details of the operation – such as how best to move the kids underwater, or when to reassure them – was given the opportunity to practise the subtle nuances of their role. Rick and I looked on, our confidence rising. The plan to evacuate four boys a day was coming together.

This familiarisation process was turbocharged later that day. A 3D version of Rick's notorious A2 whiteboard had been constructed at the dive base as part of a process the American Air Force referred to as a *Rehearsal Of Concept* (ROC) drill. A large, green fence had been placed around the area to shield us from the press and a length of rope detailing the guideline had been laid across the ground, linking our 'dummy' starting point at dive base to the kids waiting in chamber nine. All sorts of furniture was being used as signposts across the route, sometimes literally. Plastic chairs signified various air chambers within the caverns, while colour-coded, half-litre water bottles represented the type of assets that were set to be staged throughout Tham Luang, such as oxygen cylinders. Laminated sheets of A4 paper dangled from the line like bunting, each one denoting a different area of the cave.

With such a setup it was possible to perform a walkthrough of the operation, but we must have looked an odd bunch. In full view of each other, the divers moved one by one around the line in quick order towards the Wild Boars (another collection of plastic bottles). On cue, various support rescuers assumed their positions by the plastic chairs to facilitate cylinder changeovers.

Bumps and misunderstandings happened along the way; there was some confusion over where various air pockets were actually located. When I looked up, I noticed that the same stern faces that had briefly watched on the sidelines of the pool were now scrutinising us from the shadows. But after several dry runs and debates, collisions and readjustments, all performed with the assistance of the US Air Force, we were able to repeat the sequence without error. A clear timetable of action was established, as was the running order of divers for each day.

During this time, rehearsals of another type were taking place in the cave. The dry passages had been rigged by a team of Thai engineers and Navy SEALs with ziplines designed to speed the boys' evacuation. These ropeways were tested using a stretcher loaded with a volunteer. (It hung horizontally below the zipline as the boy would be.) This evacuation exercise from dive base was performed several times, and during a final dry run the smallest female member of the US Air Force team, Airman First Class Haley Moulton had agreed to be the casualty. The thinking was that she would be much closer in size to the boys and immediately a problem presented itself as she almost slipped through the bottom stretcher, which led to a rethink on the tension required for the securing straps. Another potential issue had been ironed out through practice.

I soon felt very appreciative of our two, slightly unorthodox rehearsal sessions. If anybody had been under any illusions as to what was expected of us, the realities of our workload and responsibilities were now crystal clear. The effort had also sharpened our understanding of process, though just as importantly, it looked to have convinced the authorities of our abilities too. There's little doubt our techniques had been viewed with a healthy dollop of scepticism at first. But without that level of preparation, plus one or two demonstrations of competence, there's every chance the mission would have been canned. Instead, we were readying ourselves for what would ultimately prove to be the most audacious rescue job of our lives.

■ ■ ■

That night, before going to bed, I spent a little time visualising the worst-case scenario: *one of the boys I'd been moving had stopped breathing*. When I imagined looking into the face mask, I visualised his eyes, magnified through the water, all glassy and lifeless; they were staring right through me. *He was gone*. I tried to experience the inevitable emotions in advance – the sense of shock; the pain of tragedy; the sensations as a wave of guilt, anger, and anxiety washed over me. Some people might have considered my actions to be a form of catastrophising, an invited self-fulfilling prophecy, or even an act of masochism that was setting me up for long-term failure. In reality, a psychological drill of this kind had long acted as a positive form of self-defence. I wanted to be ready should one of the boys die under my care during the mission, and by repeating this exercise, building up my emotional responses in advance and putting them into training, I felt ready for the horrors that might drift my way. I was filing away more plans in the library, just in case.

This was a technique I'd employed during our first few days in Tham Luang, as we'd searched for the boys. During those stormy nights, the rain hammering at the corrugated iron roof of our room, I'd imagined swimming into a chamber filled with thirteen dead bodies. They swayed and spun in the water like discarded plastic bags. I saw those same, grisly movements again on the eve of the extraction, only this time I was visualising a moment in which I'd entered a sump with a living child and exited with a corpse.

How would I continue in such an event? God, the thought of it felt desperate. Even though someone had died on me, I'd still need to get to the entrance of the cave in order to save myself, and by extension another Wild Boar the next day. We'd been instructed to bring the boys all the way out, even if they'd died in transit, but that carried a mortal risk for everyone involved. *Was it really worth dying while attempting to bring a dead person to the surface?* I was prepared to risk my life for a breathing child, no question. If I found myself in a tight spot, and it seemed feasible to do so, I was OK with being marooned in an air chamber with whichever Wild Boar I was trying to save. However, I wasn't going to kill myself by trying to bring through a boy who had already passed away. That night, I imagined myself surfacing with a dead child at dive base and absorbed the sense of shame and failure I would feel in the aftermath. My determination to avoid that situation at all costs intensified further.

There was also the fear that I might somehow lose a living boy in the murk. The lanyards and handles affixed to the kids had been designed to prevent such an incident, but there was still the slightest chance that an equipment malfunction *could* happen. In much the same way that a parachute sometimes fails from time to time, the chances were admittedly slim, but they were there nevertheless. I browsed the Library Of Plans for a solution: in such an unlikely event, I decided the smartest play would be search for the child as long as I had the air to swim us both to safety – whether that was inside the cave or dive base. Beyond that, there was really no point exhausting my entire air supply only to find the kid as my last breath expired. In that situation, both of us would have died shortly afterwards.

While this was an undeniably morbid train of thought, I felt morally comfortable with the choices I might have to make during the rescue. There would be little time to think or theorise if ever those imagined situations became a reality, but with my responses figured out in advance I'd be able to operate more effectively. Visualisation, I knew, was a powerful motivator and I was using it keenly, hoping it might push me away from failure. I felt an indescribably strong determination that, whatever the coming rescue held for the others, I would not make a mistake; that I would ensure *my* children at least would survive.

Meanwhile there was also the grisly business of sedation to consider. Harry had agreed to administer the ketamine from inside the cave, but his work stopped with the injections, and in doing so he was already putting his medical career on the line. But no matter how difficult the journey out with the boys proved, I wouldn't have swapped places with him for anything – I hated the thought of sedating those kids, even though there was no other option.

Unfortunately, I'd have to involve myself in the process from time to time. Given the journey from chamber nine to dive base was taking us around four hours, Harry's initial dose of sedative was almost certain to wear off before the boys in transit had been moved to safety. They would begin to stir in very distressing circumstances. This meant everyone involved would have to be prepared to administer further, top-up doses and so all the divers needed a training session on the intricacies of intramuscular injections. When we arrived for our briefing, Harry had laid out an intimidating line of syringes for us to use.

As a trained first aider with around twelve years of experience at the time, I was fairly familiar with some of the more squeamish aspects of delivering an injection – in theory anyway. During a number of courses, the practice of giving an intramuscular injection had been explained to me, in case I had to use one during a cave rescue. But rather than performing the injection on a real, live person, I remember we'd rehearsed on an orange. The reasons for this were fairly obvious at the time: an orange has a slightly tougher, exterior skin with a pulpy 'flesh' underneath, which feels similar to a human, and during those first-aid programmes, I'd made light of the situation by drawing a smiley face on the fruit with a marker pen. When faced with the prospect of administering a shot of ketamine to a semi-conscious boy in Tham Luang, the jokes quickly evaporated.

Everyone was uncomfortable. As Harry presented a bare essentials course on delivering the shots, I was able to treat the lessons as a refresher exercise. For some of the others, it must have felt terrifyingly new. Our anxieties were heightened further by the fact that all we had to practise on were plastic water bottles. There were no smiley oranges in sight.

'What does it feel like when injecting a person for the very first time, Harry?' I asked, my needle slipping into the plastic.

'Oh, well the first time you do it, you'll probably shit yourself,' he said, smiling. 'But once you've got the first one done, you'll be as right as rain.'

I trusted Harry's opinion. During the brief time we'd worked together, a bond had undoubtedly grown between us – he, too, felt an incredible sense of ownership for rescuing the Wild Boars. His broad Australian accent and down-to-earth demeanour also helped to add a little levity to the occasion, and by the end of the session everybody had been handed a waterproof kit bag containing syringes, needles and ketamine, with doses labelled *Big Kid* and *Small Kid*. (Though thankfully, these were changed to one-size-fits-all, medium doses after day one.) We were now staring down the barrel of a risk-loaded rescue.

VISUALISATION: PROCESS AND PAIN

A lot has been written about the process of visualisation, especially within fields where a focus on the desired, winner-takes-all result is vital. (Think sport, business, or endurance events.) In such cases, people are encouraged to keep their eye on the prize, or to imagine a lap of victory, in an approach that is not dissimilar to a donkey being led along by a carrot dangling from the end of a stick. Sure, it's a style of inspiration that works for some. The autobiographies of sports stars, adventurers and business leaders are full of moments of crippling doubt where some imagined spoils of success have then driven them on. But I have found that this approach really doesn't work for me. From what I've heard, I am not alone in thinking this way, not least because at some level you actually have to *believe* that you can be successful. Focusing on wishy-washy moments of glory that might not actually come to anything seems to me like a waste of mental calories.

To begin with, I experience a fair amount of imposter syndrome, as a lot of people do. The very act of writing this book has caused me to feel fraudulent at times, and somewhat exposed. As a consequence, I tend to squirm a little at any event where I am the centre of attention, so picturing the rewards of success or a moment of glory as a motivating device doesn't work. I don't want to imagine myself standing in front of a cheering audience with a gold medal around my neck. The thought of an applauding crowd of peers as I collect an *Employee of the Year Award* leaves me cold. I'd much prefer that my efforts were driven by the joy of process and technique rather than any potential rewards or accolades.

I have also found that focusing on nothing more than the end game can be joyless and rather counter-productive – simply visualising future moments of success and satisfaction can create a false sense of security, while the reality of what is actually required to succeed remains in the psychological shadows. Instead, I tend to focus my attentions on the actions and techniques required to reach that successful outcome. Then I'll imagine them in detail, whether they're positive or negative. Having visualised what needs to be done and how, I'm ready to negotiate the practical stages as and when they arrive for real.

For instance, before a dive, I will picture myself in a positive place. I'll feel myself moving through the water: I can see currents roiling around me, my hand on the line, the waft of my fins as I glide forward. From the comfort of my armchair, I am taking a positive and low-impact training session, where all the skills I might need to reach my target are committed to memory. Professional golfers are understandably obsessed with the concept of process and think in much the same way. Before every shot, they'll stand behind the ball and create the perfect swing in their mind. Having imagined the sweet sensation as club and ball connect, their shot then arcs upwards into the air and surges towards its intended target, landing softly on the green and rolling steadily towards the hole.

This technique works well in all manner of situations. A case in point: when imagining an important exam, such as a driving test, it's more helpful to visualise the techniques required to perform the perfect three-point turn, or a successful parallel parking manoeuvre, than to imagine the examiner as they congratulate you on your success at the end. Likewise, diets, or nutrition plans can fail psychologically when people look past the rituals required to succeed. Instead, they constantly dream of eating chocolate at the finish line (driving the very behaviour they want to avoid). However, by training their attention on new cooking skills, or the interest of creating a menu of delicious and nutritionally rewarding dinners, it's possible to make the process more enjoyable and draw the desired result into reality more effectively.

In a complicated diving exploration, I'll often visualise the processes in play, such as exactly where I have to stage, or switch various gas cylinders. In each case, I'll see myself executing the task perfectly. Rebreathers, for example, demand great respect. In open water there is a lot to consider when using one, and plenty can go wrong, but deep underground, divers are usually much further from home. (And by home, I mean safety.) Rebreathers contain chemicals that absorb exhaled carbon dioxide. When these chemicals are exhausted, or the diver breathes too quickly, the CO_2 level in the system increases in a runaway effect in which the additional CO_2 can cause the diver to pant. This creates anxiety, which, in turn, forces a diver to breathe even harder, until eventually they fall unconscious. Unable to swap mouthpieces, they will inevitably drown.

This horrific situation can be avoided by changing to a safe or bailout form of gas in advance, and I have often prepared for such a worst-case scenario in my recurring visualisations. I imagine vividly the uncontrollable panting and a growing sense of anxiety. I try to feel the vice-like clutch of fear around my throat and a desperate desire to swap regulators, even though I am unable to remove the rebreather mouthpiece. On hundreds of occasions I've even visualised wrestling with the very human urge to keep panting, while reaching for an imaginary spare regulator hanging round my neck. In my mind I have then pressed the purge button*, creating a pillow of air beneath my face. The bad mouthpiece is then thrown away as I choke and splutter, safely, into the new regulator.

It's also important to visualise and psychologically rehearse, for scenarios that we have grown accustomed to handling with ease. Often it's all too easy to forget the pain endured during our past successes because the brain has a tremendous capacity for gifting us with rose-tinted spectacles. A good example would be the 100-mile (160-kilometre) race, or ultra-marathon, where the completion rate for people on their second run is often lower than those runners striving to complete an ultra-marathon for the very first time.

The reason for this is very simple: when taking on such a gruelling challenge, first-timers arrive with a readied state of mind. They know the experience is set to be intense; there is a very good chance they might collapse way before the finishing line, and so they do everything they can in training to avoid failure. They run right; they eat right; they prepare right. On the day of the race, they use every trick in the book to locate extra

---

* The purge button, which is positioned on the second stage of a regulator, causes air to rush from the device. This is normally used to clear water in the mouthpiece so a diver can breathe safely from it again.

sources of motivation, internal and external, and their friends and family will line the course and shout words of encouragement. *There's a novelty factor.*

Eventually, after crossing the line, a sense of achievement kicks in. They think, '*I did it,*' but for many people it's easy to forget how they were pushed to the edges of their capacity. Complacency strikes. (And I know all about this, having competed in a number of ultra-marathons.) When the time arrives to train for a second race, they forget the intense pain of running incredibly long distances – and they quit. Or they lose sight of just how difficult a race of that kind can be – and skip training. Having thought only of the fact that they completed the test last time around, the gruelling psychological effort required to succeed is blocked out – and they fail.

What I am suggesting is quite the opposite. *We should remember the pain.* In much the same way a successful football manager might tell his team to forget the last cup final win, or any glories from the previous season – because another very different campaign is about to begin – so the ultra-marathon runner should put aside the glow of completion when committing to a new race. Rather than thinking, 'I'm an ultra-marathon runner now, I can do it,' they might do better to recall those moments when failure seemed likely. They should picture the times when, 70 miles into the last attempt, they dropped to their hands and knees in agony and puked their guts up. Or staggered towards the finish, their feet bleeding. These painful moments are strong psychological markers, as are the intervals during a race when their mind wanders to its darkest places.

Then, having relived all that discomfort and effort before their training programme begins, they can recall how they were able to summon the strength to succeed when difficulties arose last time around:

I got through this before. I know how it feels . . .

. . . And I can do it again.

The agony won't come as shock that way. The emotional distress is expected. And the gruelling effort required for running 100 miles (160 kilometres) arrives as no real surprise.

REHEARSE. THEN REPEAT: THE CHECKLIST

- Understand your plan. Practise, practise, practise.
- Visualise your feelings. Rehearse your reactions.
- Recall the pain of success. Acknowledge the effort required.

LESSON #12

MAKE SUCCESS A HABIT

In any walk of life it's important we see our commitments through to the end and then turn the process of completion into a habit. It's one of the reasons why certain business figures rise at 5 a.m. and then stay up until midnight – they are keenly focused on advancing their company, or project, and they want to accomplish again and again, over and over. While I'm not advocating such an unhealthy sleeping routine, there are rituals that we can adapt from individuals of this kind. Wanting to succeed, disliking the thought of failure, and sticking resolutely to a challenge are key traits we can all throw into our toolbox, because they're applicable to every aspect of our day to day – at work, in the gym, even at home. As I was to discover, they would function just as well in Tham Luang where I exhausted every last reserve of strength to see the rescue through . . .

DAY THIRTEEN
SUNDAY 8 JULY 2018

The mood was up. The rescue team was raring to go, but I simply couldn't understand the rush of optimism that was bouncing about the place. According to weather forecasts, more rainstorms were on the way, which meant the clock was ticking. I found it impossible to shake the dreadful feeling that we were engaged in a race against time, and that in our eagerness to save thirteen people we might just kill them all. Major 'Charlie' Charles Hodges, the US Mission Commander for the 353rd Special Operations Unit of the Air Force sensed my concern. He stepped up with a vaguely reassuring pep talk.

'John, without your help, those kids are as good as dead anyway,' he said.

While I appreciated his logic, I worried how a tragedy or death under my watch might affect me emotionally over the coming hours and days, and even in the long term. I worked to harden my resolve with a private pep talk of my own:

Yeah, the process might be risky. Some of the kids might not survive, but the boys I'm caring for absolutely will make it through.

Steadying my inner conviction was a vital first step. With a start time of 10 a.m. confirmed, there was no room for doubt and even less room for confusion. Rick, Jason and Chris, plus our support divers, gathered together and talked through the order of events once more.

Three days.

Four boys are coming out on day one; another four on day two; then four on the final day, plus the coach.

Jason goes in first and swims his Wild Boar to dive base in chamber three.

Then John.

Next up is Chris. Rick will wait in chamber eight and head in last with any medical notes for Harry on how the sedations are working out. With the help of Craig, he can assess whether the dosages are too big, too small or spot on.

This final detail was important. We hoped to fine-tune our experimental (and very worrying) medical procedures as quickly as possible if we were to extract all the Wild Boars before another storm struck. Everybody knew what they were doing; when the moment to swim towards chamber nine arrived, there was nothing in the way of fanfare. Jason dropped into the waters at dive base and then disappeared from view.

'Oh fuck,' I thought. *'Me next . . .'*

The journey to the Wild Boars' temporary home was as gruelling as ever. Handily, the cave appeared to be in a more agreeable mood and the waters had lowered further, but I was in no doubt that an incoming weather system might increase their ferocity almost immediately. Having arrived at chamber nine in one piece, it was a relief to see that the operation had taken on a life of its own. So far, events were running exactly as planned. Four boys were in varying stages of preparation, but I had no idea who was coming out first and how the decision had been arrived at. Harry had left the organisation of a timetable up to the Wild Boars themselves and a short meeting had taken place on the bank. A departure list was prepared.

From what I could tell, Coach Ek had decided that those from the neighbourhood of Ban San Wiang Hom should be the first out. They lived the farthest away, after all, and therefore imagined they would have the longest cycle ride home for food. That meant Note, Tern, Nick and Night were coming out first. It was a very sweet suggestion of Ek's, but also a telling sign that none of the stranded kids, or their responsible adult, had the faintest clue as to the emergency services, military personnel and international media ranged outside the cave. Jason had already dressed Note and taken him for sedation. Assisted by Harry, the first unconscious passenger was placed into the water; the boy's buoyancy jacket and full-face mask were securely fastened. There was no turning back for him now.

When I looked around, the SEALs were helping two more boys on the bank as they wriggled into their wetsuits. Each wore a neoprene hood packed with foam padding to further protect their heads. (Wearing a caving helmet was impossible because the boys' diving masks covered the entire face.) But the most chilling detail was the plastic cable ties that had been wrapped around the wrist of each passenger – the kind you might see attached to prisoners in a war film, or police drama. Though they weren't yet snapped together, the boys' arms had to be bound behind their backs with a karabiner once the sedation had kicked in, and while this might have seemed inhumane, the restraints were in place so that the passenger's arms and hands would stay secure during the journey. Dangling free, their limbs might become caught, or even snap against a rock. Worse, if the keta-mine was to wear off while one of the boys was still underwater, he might tear at his face mask in a sudden panic. The Wild Boars giggled as they watched their mates being dressed for what would be an incredibly dangerous journey. *It was like a game to them.*

Medically, our plan was running smoothly. Each boy had been given a Xanax tranquilliser prior to being sedated. That way he would be suitably relaxed for his ketamine injection fifteen minutes later. Harry was now on the bank, perched some way in the water, the next passenger sitting upon his knee. *My passenger.* A syringe was stuck into both legs, straight through the wetsuit – one shot of ketamine as a sedative; the other a shot of atropine, which was often administered to dry up a patient's saliva during surgical procedures. While drowning in floodwater was the biggest threat to the boys in Tham Luang, we feared they could just as easily choke on their own saliva. Every dose was calculated through educated guesswork. Harry sized up his patients expertly and judged their shot based on size and weight, taking into account possible dehydration and malnutrition.

The boy seemed relaxed in his company. Having spent a number of years working as an anaesthetist, Harry had clearly built up a reassuring bedside manner, and whenever one of the boys looked up nervously, he asked him about football, or sport. Because of his Aussie accent, Harry's jokes were landing well.

'You've got John taking you out,' he said.

John? The boy looked confused.

'Yes. *Lucky you!* He's the best one . . .' continued Harry.

There was a nervous smile.

Over the coming days, Harry would repeat the same trick for every boy, with Jason, Rick and Chris being given the same pseudo-praise as they received their injections. His chatty demeanour helped to put the Wild Boars at ease, though it probably also went some way to keeping his own stresses under control. We were all experiencing them.

I watched from the sidelines as the ketamine did its work. The passenger's eyes glazed, and then drooped, before closing over. *He was out cold.*

'He's all yours, John,' said Harry, supporting the boy as we moved him into the water.

The mask was placed over his face. It covered his eyes, nose, mouth and chin like a Perspex bubble. The passenger's head was immediately airtight; the built-in regulator provided the oxygen he needed to breathe, and he was able to inhale freely from the attached cylinder. Then came the most uncomfortable safety check of all: carefully, I pushed the kid's face underwater for several seconds, checking for any leaks or cracks in the mask seal. The very act felt horrific, and I hated it.

My anxiety was rising now. Peering down at the passenger's lifeless body, I noticed he had stopped breathing and the tell-tale signs of a functioning air cylinder, those tiny bubbles that rose through the water in ribbons, were nowhere to be seen. Maybe the cold water had shocked his lungs? Or perhaps it had something to do with the ketamine? I really didn't know. Trying to remain calm I pressed the purge button on his regulator in an attempt to force more oxygen into his lungs. *Nothing.* I pressed again. *Still no response.*

'Oh no,' I thought looking up at Harry nervously. 'This is not good.'

Finally, after a few seconds, the boy seemed to relax. I spotted the first curlicue of air in the water and puffed out a sigh of relief. He was exhaling.

It's OK . . .

. . . Now for the tricky bit.

There was no backing out now, though I desperately wanted to. The thought of swimming for over 1.5 kilometrs (1 mile) through churning water currents and scrambling over rocky terrain – somehow without killing the child in my care – filled me with dread. I strapped the air cylinder to the passenger's chest and positioned him face down in the water once more; his buoyancy jacket was holding him on the surface. I then attached the cargo to my harness with a lanyard so he wouldn't float away into the dark at any point. My safety checks complete, I swam towards the tunnels, pushing and pulling the lifeless body along with me.

I felt stressed. My stomach knotted; the muscles around my Adam's apple had constricted a little. *Was I experiencing stage fright?* Everything was moving so fast and yet my subconscious was telling me to slow down, or at least to maintain some form of emotional control. *But how?* The rescue had taken on a momentum all of its own, and in double-quick time, so there was no room for a time-out, or some moment of silent contemplation. And then a thought struck me. *I didn't know which boy I was swimming with.* Where that sudden urge to identify who I was rescuing had come from, I'm not entirely sure, because previously it had felt important to protect the other divers from becoming too attached to the kids as they swam into chamber nine with food, supplies or notes. Meanwhile, I wasn't entirely sure who was who – I hadn't got to know the kids by their names. My need for connection wasn't sentimental either. Instead, I wanted to remind myself that the package I was about to transport, while being very much inert, was a human being, *and just a kid*. More importantly, he was also a son, a friend and maybe even a brother to any number of people waiting anxiously beyond the cave.

I shouted back to Chris on the bank.

'What's his name?'

But Chris didn't know, and it was too late to lean down and ask. The poor kid had already been sedated. I would have to do without.

I learned later, after the first day of rescues, that my passenger was Tern. He was slight of build and I was glad to be transporting one of the smaller boys – physically it would make my work a little easier. Whenever I had visited the Wild Boars in chamber nine, Tern had always appeared full of life, despite being stuck in a gloomy cave with no light, no comforts and not much in the way of decent food. I remembered his big smile.

As we moved further and further away from the bank and the watching boys, a funny thing happened. My anxiety was instantly outweighed by a feeling of loneliness, one I hadn't experienced during the operation so far. Face down in the water I could see the murk shifting and shimmering as sediment flows churned this way and that. I heard the sound of percolating air bubbles and felt the wash of water in my ears. But none of those experiences were new or unusual. Nor was the weight of Tern's lifeless body as I carried him alongside me – the bags of supplies I had transported into the Wild Boars previously had been just as heavy.

What *was* different this time around was the burden of responsibility – and it felt crushing. Tern's survival was all on me; I was beyond the reach of Harry and medical help, and that was a massive psychological weight to carry. I didn't feel entirely comfortable about it, either. Having glanced down, the flesh of Tern's palms, now bound together behind his back, suddenly seemed so very pale in the glare of my torchlight, his soles too. It reminded me of just how vulnerable the boy was in the water. I did my best not to scrape his feet along the bottom of the cave, though my main concern was to protect the seal of his face mask.

If a head cracked against the roof at any point, it had to be my head. If a face mask were to dislodge in the currents, it would have to be my face mask. Keeping the boy breathing was my top priority.

The feeling of isolation was so powerful that I felt slightly envious of Tern's sedated state. A Xanax would have gone some way to smoothing off the ragged emotional edges. It also might have helped to referee the strange wrestling match taking place inside my head. Part of me very much accepted the realities of our situation; I understood that it was my job to get three boys out of the Tham Luang caves over the next few days, and that I had been given the task, alongside Rick, Jason and Chris, because we were the divers best placed to execute the mission.

'It's right that I'm doing this,' I told myself. *'Who else could do it?'*

But experience also made me keenly aware of the consequences were I to make a mistake at any point. Which is probably why the early symptoms of imposter syndrome were beginning to emerge.

'I don't want to be here,' I thought. *'I want to be out of it.'*

I attempted to pump the brakes on what was fast becoming a runaway train of negative thoughts, and kicked forward.

Do the job . . . And do it well.

The first sump of our fraught journey together was coming into view. Releasing a little air from Tern's buoyancy jacket, I pushed him forward into the deeper waters. There was zero resistance. It was like moving a corpse, and with one hand on the line, I submerged him into the black, his body beneath mine. I had chosen to cradle the passenger's head beneath my chin – *I had to protect him from the rocky knuckles above* – and we progressed for around twenty minutes. At intervals I peered down to check the boy was still breathing by counting the time between his exhalations. Given his position, a small stream of bubbles appeared in front of my face mask with every gasp of air; they really were the only sign of life. And worryingly, the intervals between breaths were undoubtedly lengthening; time seemed to be slowing. Every now and then, I feared that Tern's lungs might have stopped working altogether. Unable to remove his mask, I'd press at the purge button on his regulator, hoping to force a little oxygen into his chest, my stress spiking until the tell-tale bubbles drifted past my face once more.

Tension was building. More than anything, I wanted to avoid the distressing exchanges of condolence that would have to take place if he died. The idea of being introduced to Tern's parents – had he stopped breathing under my care – and then having to express my sorrow and regret would have been too painful to bear. *I'm so sorry for your loss.* Just the thought of saying those words left me feeling desolate, and my every ounce of strength was going to be needed to ensure it didn't happen. I pushed him even further into the deep and pressed on.

■ ■ ■

There was a shape in the water ahead.

As it moved closer, the shadowy silhouette of a diver came into view and I soon recognised the face mask. *It was Rick!* But there was no time to stop and wave a cheery hello or communicate further. Instead, we passed on the line in a well-rehearsed move, shifting our hands around each other without once losing contact with the rope. As he crossed, Rick flashed me the OK sign and peered down at Tern's lifeless body. Then I noticed the confused look on his face. Apparently, Rick had assumed, wrongly, that I would wait in chamber nine until his arrival, especially as he was in possession of some important medical feedback on the state of the first boy. But our wires had been crossed and once Harry had sedated Tern, I was committed. As we parted, I knew that Rick's appearance was confirmation that Jason had made it to the first dry stretch of the rescue. *But had the kid survived, too?* Rick's expression made it impossible to tell.

Things were changing ahead of me. The water was becoming a little clearer. And as I reached forward, I noticed that the blue guideline was coming to an end and had been knotted to a thick, red climbing rope, which meant we were approaching the first dry section of the trip, the swirl cavern of chamber eight. If all went to plan, Craig Challen and Claus from the Euro team would be waiting to assist us over the rocks and into the next sump. It would also give us an opportunity to check on Tern's breathing and to make sure he wasn't regaining consciousness

The floor was changing below me: water gave way to sand; sand gave way to cobbles and gravel; until, eventually, I was able to float Tern to one side. The passage was low and wide, and there was very little room above – I needed to feel my way forward so as not to smash the boy's face into the rising gravel shelf. *But I was fast running out of hands!* One gripped the line, the other held on to the boy, but knowing that Tern's body couldn't drift away, I released my hold on the line, reaching ahead until I was able to feel the arch that would lead us to where Claus and Craig were supposed to be waiting with a stretcher.

But Craig wasn't there. There was no sign of Claus either. I looked this way and that, my torch beaming about the cavern, but we were still terrifyingly alone. I shouted out. *Had Craig and Claus got lost? Or worse, had Jason's boy been injured or drowned?*

But there was no time for speculation; I had to heave Tern from the water. I carefully shifted his body on to the shingle beach before resting him in the recovery position, and removed his mask. *Please be breathing.* I tilted his head back, and leant close, listening for some small indication of life. Finally, it was possible to feel a faint and shallow sigh on my cheek. Tern was still alive, *thank heavens.* And then I heard the crunch of footsteps behind me. Craig had finally showed.

'All good?' he said, looking down at Tern.

I nodded. 'I think so. He's still breathing. *Where's Claus?*'

Craig shrugged and set to work on Tern as I lugged my equipment towards the next sump. By all accounts, the first dive was going well. Craig had just helped Jason on his way and Note seemed to be in once piece. Fretfully, I watched the medical assessment taking place, feeling amazed that a full-time vet, who was more versed in caring for sick household pets than children, could appear so confident and at ease when assessing a heavily sedated boy in a cave. Having become certain that Tern was fine, we manhandled him towards the next dive pool. I grabbed his hands; Craig held his feet, and we took care not to bump him on any rocks or sharp outcrops.

Suddenly there was a noise. Claus had finally arrived with the stretcher.

'Where the fuck have you been?' I shouted, my patience snapping.

Claus mumbled an excuse. I apologised and we settled down to business – I had given Claus an unfairly hard time, but he had been unsure of where to meet us, and I had very little time for excuses. I was emotionally and physically strained; my patience was frayed, and our circumstances seemed incredibly trying. This was no time for tardiness, but there was very little room for a dispute, either. I bit my tongue as the three of us loaded Tern onto the stretcher and moved him to the next diving section. Aware that the clock was ticking, I sealed the boy's mask tightly and pressed ahead. Moments later, we were submerged and moving purposefully. The world was dark once more; the only indication of life from my passenger was the occasional plume of air from his regulator mask; the only sound the muffled gurgle of bubbles as I exhaled. Loneliness had returned.

At that point, I had been swimming in and out of the cave for around ten days. The caverns and tunnels at the farthest end of Tham Luang, where the boys had been stranded, felt more familiar than ones we had repeatedly explored during the early phases of our search operation. As the guidelines changed colour ahead of me, I began recognising various ropes from my second week of diving in Thailand. We were making real progress and I was able to count down the landmarks and features around us: the body boards pinned to the roof of the cave; a length of black rope here, a stalagmite there. *We were well on our way home.*

Though there were still two hours to go, some rush of excitement would have been excusable. No one would have blamed me for wanting to increase my urgency in getting Tern out of the water. However, I knew that Jason wasn't too far ahead, the last thing I wanted was to swim into a huge cloud of sediment or detritus wafted up by his fins. I had also envisioned a situation where we both arrived in the next air space at exactly the same time. With the support divers' attempting to switch two set of cylinders simultaneously, there was every chance that some terrible mistake might happen. Having come so far with Tern, the last thing I wanted was for a flash of impatience to result in an accident. I slowed my momentum and maintained a steady pace, eventually arriving in chamber six, where Erik Brown and Ivan Karadzic were waiting.

When putting together the *Inert Package Plan*, we had decided that this point in the rescue would provide each lead diver with a few minutes of rest. And while I was certainly exhausted, the idea of relinquishing responsibility for Tern, even for the briefest of moments, felt wrong. He was *my* passenger, *my* responsibility. We had come so far together, and I felt desperately protective. The thought of someone else moving him into the next stretch of water, out of my reach, was unimaginable. *Was I a control freak?* At that moment, yes – 100 per cent. I swapped out my depleted air cylinder for a full tank and carried Tern onwards into what was an open canal, swimming us towards chambers five and four. The boy, amazingly, was still sleeping peacefully.

We were nearly home. And nothing bad was going to happen on my watch.

I felt fiercely determined about that.

■ ■ ■

I could feel the current behind me now. I used it to propel us gently towards chambers five and four – some of the toughest sections of Tham Luang. At this point, the line funnelled through complicated squeezes and around rock formations as the visibility deteriorated further. Smashing into a rock with a spine-cracking bang was scary enough when travelling solo, but with an unconscious boy cradled in my arms, the associated risks had increased considerably. I feared that if I was forced to one side while wriggling through a gap in the rock, I might accidentally knock Tern's head on a limestone wall or dislodge his mask at a point where I was ten or twenty minutes away from the nearest air space. The visibility in this part of Tham Luang was also next to zero, the sediment obscuring it as a result of the countless dives into this section of the cave throughout the week. Losing my grip on the line at any point would prove nightmarish and I might never rediscover it. The stakes had been raised considerably.

Even in the dark, I knew of the dangers lurking nearby. The left wall was scarred with a jagged stalactite formation and I reached out for the toothy surface, knowing it was an early sign of the struggle to come: just ahead, the tunnels pinched in, and though I was capable of pulling Tern through relatively unscathed, a series of dead, plastic glow sticks, set by divers during the rescue effort's first few days, still dangled from the guideline like oversized clothes pegs. Each one made for an unwelcome obstacle as I twisted this way and that, forced forward by the thrumming current.

My heart pounded. Though I couldn't see anything ahead of me, I knew that the safest way when negotiating this tricky stretch of terrain was to swim to the roof of the cave. Once above the guideline, it would be possible for me to feed Tern through a hole in the rock wall ahead. As my lights reflected uselessly in the heavy brown silt, I wasn't able to see it, but I knew roughly where it should be, and by feeling my way along the stalactites and outcrops I reached towards the gap. Every grab was painful. Throughout these ten days in the caves, my hands had been cut and scraped to a pulp. I hadn't worn any gloves during my dives so far – the water was warm-*ish*, and in the dark I had gained a more telling feel on the rock without them as I tried to read the walls like Braille. But a series of lacerations on my knuckles had left my flesh raw. The wounds had become pulpy and infected from the dirty water, and I was now paying the painful price.

I found the hole – *finally*. The time had come for the hard work to start. Warily, I pushed Tern ahead, careful not to catch his mask on any stalactites, and having nudged his body forwards, I followed in behind, shoving gently until we were both into a larger expanse of water. Without looking too closely, I knew we had landed in the fourth chamber and both of us seemed to be in good shape. Importantly, our cylinders still contained more than enough gas to get us home. I popped my head briefly above the water and then submerged once more, feeling my way forward in the dark, trying not to pull on the rope for fear of dislodging it, all the while keeping a careful eye out for the left turn that would signify the home stretch towards dive base. Once past it, the surface would be only 50 metres (160 feet) away.

Really, the hardest work had been done. As long as the bubbles drifting up from Tern's mask remained steady, he would probably survive what had been a grim ordeal. Though he had been an unknowing passenger, the poor boy had probably taken one or two bumps and scrapes to his arms and legs. Meanwhile, I was bloody knackered – physically and emotionally. My muscles ached; my brain wanted to drift away into a long and restful sleep, and my ears and sinuses throbbed from yet another building infection. What had started as a head cold was now a pounding face-ache, another consequence of ten days spent working in filthy water. I had survived so far on decongestants and a snort of nasal spray every couple of hours. It wasn't ideal; I would very much suffer in the coming days, but there was no way I was bailing out on the rescue mission now.

The junction came and went, the floor of the cave rose up to meet us and I could feel the mud and pebbles beneath me as I dragged Tern forward. *Chamber three and dive base weren't too far away. From there the military would whisk him away for medical treatment.* And then, unexpectedly, my passenger felt incredibly heavy. He wouldn't move. I pulled gently on the strap attached to his back in an attempt to edge him towards safety, careful not to compromise his mask, but he remained steadfast. Tern was bloody stuck. *And now of all places!* I tried again, yanking harder this time, but whatever was holding the boy in place had grabbed him tight. I felt edgy once more. Though our cylinders were over half full, a lengthy process of digging or untangling someone in such a vulnerable and exposed position as Tern might take some time, especially if I was to avoid injuring him. The comfort zone of air in both our tanks would diminish very quickly.

I looked down. It was impossible to see past Tern's shoulders in the swirling, brown waters, so there was no option other than to park him at the bottom of the chamber, but that was a delicate process. Taking care that the cylinder affixed to his chest would stop his face and regulator from plunging into the mud and rock below, I unclipped the passenger from my body and secured him to the line. Now able to move freely, I patted him down like a nightclub bouncer, until I located the cause of his problem: a length of old black telephone wire had wrapped around his right calf and was lassoing him to the spot. Thankfully, the lines were decommissioned, so I wouldn't have to manage them with too much caution. Instead, I made two cuts with my shears, and slowly pulled Tern free, before carefully looping my arm over the guideline and reattaching him to my harness. The last thing I had wanted was to lose contact with our route to dive base, especially as we were less than five minutes away. The hum of water pumps was growing louder. Our journey was done.

My head broke the surface. The lights of chamber three felt

glaring, and I was struck by the intense activity moving around us. Even before I had surfaced, my spasmodic jerks on the line as it broke surface had been noticed. I heard shouting and the announcement that a diver had returned safely. *Fish on!* Several pairs of hand reached down to pull the boy from the water. And then a well-practised chain of events fell into place in which Tern was hauled free, hoisted on to a stretcher and checked over before being dragged away by ropes. I barely had time to unclip. If I hadn't, there's every chance I'd have been dragged along with him, such was the urgency in getting him to treatment.

One of the US Air Force rescue team leant down to help.

'Is he alive?' I asked.

He nodded. *Yes.*

Relieved, I collapsed back into the water, dragged down by the weight of my gas cylinders. I had done all I could for the boy. The diving was finished. We had negotiated all the flooded sections. Now he was out of my hands as he started his journey through the dry parts of the cave.

I was emotionally spent and utterly exhausted. My mind was under siege, too. As I watched Tern's body disappear around the corner, the intense loneliness that had struck me inside chamber nine returned. Only twelve divers had been allowed into the cave beyond chamber three, to simplify what was still a dangerous rescue plan. An army of military personnel, medical staff, and volunteers were now working between the dive base and the entrance and were moving the child on; all of them focused on Tern's wellbeing, and rightly so. Still, it was hard not to feel invisible. I sat in the water and gathered myself together. *Was I really expected to make the same trip tomorrow? And the next day?* The thought of it was bruising. But stepping down wasn't an option.

I looked around for support. Jason, ever the consummate professional, was nowhere in sight: having safely delivered his boy, he had decided to begin his preparations for another intense rescue dive the following day. That was how he worked, and I respected it. But Chris and Rick were due to appear at any moment, that's if everything had gone to plan. They would need some help when getting out of the water; their cylinders would take some dragging up the bank. I really didn't want them to experience the same heavy mood of abandonment that had overwhelmed me, especially if tragedy struck either of their passengers. It was one thing to feel alone having successfully rescued a boy. Rising up in the water with a corpse could prove psychologically devastating.

One by one, the divers appeared, their imminent arrival signalled by a gurgle of bubbles in the sump and the twitching of the line. Their shadows seemed to ripple; it was possible to spot the masks and air cylinders as two figures sharpened into focus beneath the surface – rescuer and rescued. Chris arrived first, looking drained. The trip had taken its toll. Rick showed up soon after, acting as if it had been just another routine exploration. Then our support divers came in, until eventually, Harry's head popped above the water.

'How did we do?' he shouted anxiously.

Four for four!

His face dropped. Harry looked frazzled. 'Fuck, mate . . . *We killed them all?*'

No, they all survived!

Harry smiled. The look of relief was telling. Nobody could quite believe we'd gone and bloody done it.

Having relived this episode over and over, there is little doubt in my mind that the mission would have been scrapped, had one of the boys been killed that day. Thankfully, everyone had come through, and so the authorities were happy for us to proceed. We stripped out of our wetsuits and checked over the masks and equipment in preparation for our next dive the following morning. Unbelievably, the air reserves that had been staged throughout the cave were barely dented. With support divers due to take in replacements, there would be sufficient resources for the next forty-eight hours and our opening day's efforts could be repeated without a huge resupplying effort. Our only concern now was how to keep the next four boys alive. But to do so, we would have to make a habit of our opening day's success.

THE GAMIFICATION OF SUCCESS

One way of driving habitual success is to use the travelator theory, as discussed in Lesson #1, by first taking the simplest steps towards whatever end goal we're striving for, *but with diligence*. This might be the downloading of the correct application letter for a business grant, or a phone call to the estate agents in the exact area we want to move to. These actions might feel like tiny steps in an otherwise huge commitment; however by stepping aboard the travelator with extreme care, and therefore breaking the challenge into significantly smaller and manageable chunks, we need only complete the next seemingly tiny task to advance. And the next. *And the next*. Before we know it, serious progress has been made.

Sometimes a commitment can take its toll, though. The

process becomes boring; the travelator feels slow – it might even grind to a halt. One painstaking and time-consuming activity I engage in before every dive is the preparing of each and every aspect of my equipment with an exceptionally high level of diligence. Although it's a relatively easy process, it is also one with a large number of steps, and it would be very easy to skip some, or to cut corners. But that's a risk I'm not prepared to take. While I have often made jokes about wanting a 'caving butler', someone on hand to prepare my equipment for me, the truth is I would be unwilling to delegate these tasks. Cave exploration has taught me that no matter how experienced a diver is, if they haven't looked after their kit correctly, it's unlikely to look after *them* inside the cave. Taking these steps is my key to success and I repeat them habitually.

A more relatable example for most of us might be the introduction of a new nutrition plan, a commitment that can sometimes feel almost impossible during the early phases. After all, who really wants to embark on six weeks of reduced carbs and minimal sugar? But if a dieter plans and prepares their meal plans and batch cooks in advance with diligence, they'll find the overall challenge easier to manage.

Of course, executing procedures of this kind are easier said than done, which is where the concept of *gamification* comes in to play. I first heard the term in 2008, and it has since come to signify the idea of bringing fun or rewarding elements into an otherwise mundane or difficult event, examples of which include education, rehabilitation, work productivity, exercise, responsible spending and that tricky nutrition plan. The key to gamification's success centres upon dopamine: the neurotransmitter that stimulates our brain's pleasure receptors whenever we achieve, and as a result incentivises us to concentrate, feel motivated and learn. It's the reason why so many of us get a mini 'high' after reaching a target or surpassing a previous best.

By gamifying ordinary but important tasks, we can more easily make them habitual. For example, the idea of *a winning streak* and the satisfaction in maintaining it is a facet of many computer games – it can be incredibly rewarding having maintained an impressive run of victories on *Fortnite* or the FIFA football game. But I have found that by applying the same concept to activities such as running, I am able to stick to my targets and long-term goals more easily. If my training schedule demands a certain weekly mileage, I'll keep track of my work and take great satisfaction when maintaining the programme over a series of weeks and months. The idea, though, is for the process to be fun and quietly rewarding, rather than a stick to beat myself with. The same concepts can be applied to building fitness or giving up smoking or drinking. (*Ever heard of Dry January?*) Anyone in need of assistance will find there are a host of apps that can chart our progress in whatever challenge we've embarked upon.

In Tham Luang, the work was gruelling, and the challenges were severe. Every single diver working in the caves had been exhausted by the events of the first day and it was a slog to keep going. But there was no other choice but to press ahead until the Wild Boars were safely out. I used the concept of a winning streak to maintain forward momentum throughout the extractions. *One day down, one boy rescued. Two days down, two boys rescued* . . . In much the same way that a primary school teacher might use a star chart to motivate younger pupils, so I was tracking the successes.

My style of gamification was undeniably darker, though. Rather than planning a massive celebration or attempting to draw some form of joy or satisfaction when swimming Tern to safety, I simply focused on the elements of Lesson #5. Step one: take three seconds and breathe. Step two: take three minutes and think about keeping the boy alive. Step three: take three hours and get back to dive base in one piece. All those things combined acted as a powerful motivator. My success so far had been a result of good habits – patience, commitment and due diligence. Careful preparation underpinned my confidence and propelled me forward.

MAKE SUCCESS A HABIT: THE CHECKLIST

- Gamify chores. Count winning streaks.
- Complete tasks. Don't skip the small ones.
- Create structure. Build routine.

LESSON #13

DEFINE YOUR OWN HAPPINESS

What is success? In the context of the Tham Luang operation it was the extraction of all twelve Wild Boars and their coach over three days without serious injury. This was a team effort in which I am proud to have played my part. I wanted to say, 'I did OK'. There was no need to set records, or to save all thirteen people singlehandedly. Instead I set a satisfactory target and despite some undeniable road bumps along the way, I worked steadily towards it. However, it's possible for all of us to do something similar no matter the challenge ahead because we are the gatekeepers for our benchmarks and feelings. By managing them carefully, we're able to create our own happiness levels . . .

DAY FOURTEEN
MONDAY 9 JULY 2018

Adul was out cold. He had first stirred before chamber five and having dragged him out of the water, I stuck a ketamine-loaded syringe into his thigh, just as Harry had done an hour or so previously. The needle slipped easily through his wetsuit and I could only hope that the dose had been measured accurately. My early first-aid lessons and those smiley orange faces had done nothing to prepare me for a moment such as this. Meanwhile, Harry's reassuring words that I would inevitably 'shit myself' in such a situation, only hinted at the fear I was now experiencing. I felt cold and isolated. The chamber was silent, apart from the occasional ripple and drip of water pooling about me somewhere.

A sudden noise caused me to look up. I was hyper-alert and on edge, which was unsurprising given that I'd been hunched over an unconscious boy with a syringe in my hand – I must have looked like the perpetrator of some terrible murder. As my vision adjusted to the shadows, Josh Bratchley, a British support team diver, materialised in front of me. He had been waiting for my arrival so we could move Adul into the next sump together.

'How is he?' he said, leaning down check on the boy's wellbeing. 'It's OK, Adul. It's going to be OK . . .'

The jury was still out on that one. Adul was a lot bigger than Tern. Having moved him away from the ninth cavern, where now only six boys and coach Ek – plus the Navy SEALs – had been left to wave us off cheerily, I had been struck by the boy's size; I even worried that he might prove too big for the journey. *Would I be able to squeeze the kid through the narrow gap between chambers five and four without injuring him?* But there was no time to ponder. In the end I had adjusted to my new cargo fairly quickly, cradling Adul's head under my chin and pulling him along in much the same way as I had done with Tern. We'd soon found a steady pace. Checking on the boy's condition had been a hell of a lot easier, too: Adul breathed like a steam train. Plumes of bubbles exploded around me with every exhalation. The report card from the halfway mark read: *so far, so good.*

'Yes, he's fine . . . I think,' I said.

But I had spoken too quickly. Having readied Adul for the next leg of the journey, we replaced his face mask, but something felt off. When I looked down to check, the boy had stopped breathing.

Shit! *Was he dead?* I removed the mask and ran through the same procedures as yesterday, tilting his head back, listening in close, hoping to hear or feel some faint gasp or a sign that his lungs were still functioning. But there was nothing. My heart sank. *Had I overdosed him?* I looked up at Josh in alarm. The nightmare moment had arrived, and I used my psychological rehearsals to adopt a rational approach to what was becoming a very panicked situation.

When a person falls unconscious, their hearing is the final sense to fade. That's why nurses and emergency services workers reassure their casualties with gentle words of comfort – the stricken individual might still be able to hear. Josh, in his politest voice, attempted to coax the boy back to life.

'Come on, Adul. You can do this. Breathe. *Breathe . . .*'

But I had no such patience. Guessing that my passenger wasn't going to remember anything from his near-death experience on the floor of a darkened cavern in the middle of Tham Luang, I took a more aggressive approach.

'Breathe, you fucker,' I shouted. '*Breathe!*'

Josh looked at me reproachfully, but I couldn't have cared less at that point – one of the Wild Boars, *my Wild Boar*, was potentially dying under my supervision.

'*What?*' I snapped. 'He's fucking unconscious. I don't need to be nice to him! Come on, Adul, *BREATHE!*'

Suddenly, the boy stirred and I watched as his chest rose and fell gently. Josh replaced his mask, taking care to apply the straps to the back of his head, but almost instantly Adul's lungs seemed to stop again. Removing the mask, we were then forced to wait anxiously for several seconds before the faintest of life signs returned. I couldn't believe it. Whenever the mask came off, Adul's lungs began to work. Slipped back on, they stopped. Off, breath. On, no breath. 'This isn't good,' I thought, realising we were caught between a rock and a hard place: given the boy's condition, we couldn't move on to the next phase of the rescue, but it wasn't feasible for us to remain in chamber five forever, either. We tested the mask and waited. Our only option was to give the boy a chance to sleep off some of the sedation. My mind raced. Though I had slept fairly restfully the previous night, this entire business – thirteen days in a cave, trying to find, and then rescue, a football team of children – had taken its toll. I wanted the job to be done with; emotionally I had hit my lowest ebb. For a brief moment, I even considered bolting for the exit with Adul and then I heard those three little words.

It'll be alright.

There was the warning sign. Deep down I knew it would be anything but alright and, thankfully, the urge to rush passed quickly. I had to focus on keeping Adul alive. By the looks of things, Josh understood that both a clear head and rational thinking were imperative. He made sure I knew it, too. Minutes passed, which felt like a bloody lifetime. Then Josh looked up and smiled.

'Hey, John!' he said. 'I think he's going to be OK.'

I stooped down and took a look for myself. Adul seemed more stable; his breathing was certainly steadier. Making one final check, we dragged him into the water, attached his face mask securely and watched as a current of powerful bubbles rippled around his head. *Talk about a relief!* To this day, I have no idea what might have caused the problem. Maybe the dosage measurements had been a little off? Or perhaps there was a fault with the face mask? But any technical debriefings would have to wait until the day's rescue efforts had been completed. Waving goodbye to Josh, I swam Adul gently towards chamber three and dive base, telling myself that everything was going to be just fine.

But then, everything *had* been just fine up until that moment. Certainly, nothing about the early phases of our second dive had suggested a near disaster was in the making. I had arrived at chamber nine as before; the SEALs were helping the boys into their wetsuits; and Harry was using his charm to relax the kids. ('Manchester United? Yeah mate, I support them too!') My only concern had been the weather conditions. The previous night, as we discussed our first successful rescues in the team hotel, news had reached us that the monsoon rains were due to attack us once more, probably in around a day or so. There was even a worry that the conditions might worsen to such an extent that a third day of diving would prove too treacherous. My heart sank. I really didn't want to think about the churning rapids at the cave's entrance, or the prospect of saving some of the boys, only to leave the others inside.

Somebody then raised the question of whether we could make two very quick dives in one day, but the idea was unnerving, not to mention unachievable. I was bloody knackered, and though I was still able to operate within the physical limits I usually set myself, I knew that if I went beyond those there was a chance I might make a grave mistake, especially if I pushed too hard. But I wasn't the only one feeling the strain. Rick looked tired, too. In fact, out of the group, only Jason seemed to have a spring in his step. He was a solid diver and a proactive person; Jason had a tonne of energy to burn and always seemed to be one step ahead. Having him around felt like a blessing at this stage, especially as some of us were clearly fading by the hour.

The next morning, our second dive had followed the exact same running order as the previous day: *Jason goes in first. Then John. Next up is Chris. Rick will head in last.* I soon settled into a comfy rhythm on the return journey with my precious cargo. Our team was well drilled: the support divers had restocked the cave with air cylinders, and everyone arrived in their correct positions at the appropriate time. It was only once Adul's breathing had packed up that the wheels had threatened to come off, but thankfully it was nothing more than a stressful hiccup.

We later moved smoothly through the rocky tubes that separated chamber five from four before being plucked from the waters by the ever-reliable US Air Force. Adul was carried away to the on-site field hospital and I was left to contemplate another successful package delivery. I hadn't dropped the ball. *I was doing OK.* And by the end of day two, we had rescued four more Wild

Boars. Eight had been extracted in total; there were four more to go plus Coach Ek, and nobody seemed to believe that we had been able to save everyone so far. The mood among the divers that night was one of weary optimism. For the parents, confusion: the authorities had kept secret which of the boys had been rescued and who remained inside.

But away from our group an atmosphere of international celebration was taking hold. And while I empathised with some of the emotional outpourings, we were not yet out of the woods. We passed through dive base where another round of backslapping and handshakes piled on top of us, but the well-wishing was upgraded considerably when Thailand's prime minister, Prayuth Chan-ocha then stopped by to express his gratitude. As I sat awkwardly alongside the assembled British contingent at our rickety plastic table in the encampment office, it was hard not to feel a little embarrassed. None of us were exactly ready for receiving dignitaries; the job wasn't yet done. So to deflect the attention, I clumsily introduced Bas and Tom, our minders from the local tourist police, who had looked after us so well while we had stayed in Tham Luang.

'These two,' I said, a little too enthusiastically. 'They've been brilliant, We've really appreciated their help . . .'

Both men shrank into the shadows, fearing a minor political brouhaha was about to end their careers. But judging by the reception we had received outside the cave, we seemed to be just about bulletproof – diplomatically at least. I hoped the final rescue day wouldn't put that theory to the test.

DAY FIFTEEN
TUESDAY 10 JULY 2018
- -

The clouds ruptured yet again but the mood at dive base, while not exactly upbeat, still brimmed with a quiet confidence. The waters weren't quite foaming through the early chambers as feared and a small window of time remained to extract the last four boys and their coach safely. The trapped Navy SEALs would follow us out after the silt in the water, stirred up by our movements, had settled. The running order was set to work exactly as before (it wasn't broken, so why fix it?), only this time Coach Ek – who would also be sedated – was to be brought out at the same time. In planning, Jason had offered to shuttle the coach through to chamber eight before returning to collect the last boy. Meanwhile the Belgian diver, Jim Warny, would swim Ek to the dive base. This was a little more complicated than our previous operational days, but there was nothing to suggest the load was unmanageable.

The rain was tearing at the jungle outside as the final preparations were made. I felt nervous. Having experienced situations such as this one before, it wasn't out of the question that a storm surge or sudden increase in water might lift the flood waters to a dangerous level around us. The surge would move quickly, too, and in torrents, swallowing up everything in its path. At that point, everybody would have to scramble for the exit. Given there were one or two nooks and crannies to squeeze through between dive base and the entrance, I didn't fancy being caught in a scrum with a unit of Navy SEALs and a number of burly, Australian police officers, all of whom would be in the queue ahead of us. Rick and I hung back until the last second before entering the cave. I resolved to keep an eye on the water and to swim until forward momentum became impossible once the dive had begun.

My fears were unfounded. The journey to chamber nine, though more turbulent than usual, proved uneventful. But having reached the bank where Harry was performing his final sedations, I was still concerned by the water levels in the cave. Every day, I had taken a half-litre bottle of water into chamber nine with me. This was for two reasons. The first was to rehydrate. Diving was exhausting work, and it was important to drink whenever possible.

The second reason for taking a plastic bottle into chamber nine was so we could gather information. Having guzzled the last of my water, I liked to stick the used container into the muddy bank, right at the waterline. This was a practical move rather than a shoddy attitude to littering: the markers delivered an indication as to whether the floodwaters were rising or falling over successive days. Up to that moment, the line had been retreating in chamber nine. But with the latest storm, that retreat had been halted. Water was pouring in through the tunnels and up from the rock below. There was every chance we would have to speed up the evacuation if we were to avoid any final-day dramas.

As hoped, my last run passed without too much stress, but Chris wasn't so lucky. As Rick, and I waited at dive base, concerns were raised after he failed to materialise on schedule. Chris had left not long after I had: *where was he?* It soon turned out that he had run into trouble while negotiating the churning waters that divided chambers four from three and had lost hold of his guideline, the nightmare scenario for any diver in a blind hole.

Chris moved this way and that, all the while trying to locate his bearings. Having swum with the boy for around ten minutes, he then latched on to a black cord that *might* have been the route home – except it wasn't. Instead, Chris had found an old electrical cable, the type that had ensnared Tern just forty-eight hours previously, and having followed along it for a few minutes, he arrived in an unrecognisable stretch of chamber four. Spotting a muddy bank in the distance, Chris changed course, pulling his still unconscious cargo with him. Once on dry land, he then hauled the Wild Boar up with him and removed his mask. Both of them had been bloody lucky.

The only option was to wait it out. But as Chris wrapped the boy in a foil blanket and cradled him for warmth, a voice called out. It was Rick bringing out one of the last two Wild Boars. He instructed Chris to hold tight and to wait for Harry, who was following on behind, Rick then swam on with his own passenger. Jason passed moments later, offering similar words of encouragement, and then, when Harry finally arrived, he was able to help Chris to the line, before taking charge of the boy for the final swim home. Not only had Harry handled the tricky business of sedating the boys effectively, he had been able to carry out a passenger in a moment of emergency. Fate had so nearly conspired against us at the end, but together we had brought the entire Wild Boars football team and their coach to the surface, unharmed.

A mood of celebration broke out around us at dive base. Buckets of fried chicken had been smuggled into the cave; the US Air Force passed around a bottle of Jack Daniels, but honestly, the only emotion coursing through me was an overwhelming sense of relief. I hadn't fucked up. *What more could I ask for?* Running another gauntlet of euphoric hugs, I retreated from the cave and found a quiet corner in our office encampment. Grandstanding displays and congratulatory parties had never been my thing. As far as I was concerned, the flight home to England couldn't come quickly enough. I was shattered.

The following hours became something of a blur. I remember being introduced to the parents of Tern, Adul and the final boy I'd transported to safety, Tee. Through an interpreter we made plenty of small talk, and I was happy to chat, having come to understand just how important conversations of this kind were to the families of a survivor. Those boys were precious and I'd helped avoid an awful disaster. Most of all, I felt mightily relieved not to be staring down the barrel of a tragedy: I wouldn't have to look anyone in the eye, offer my sympathies, or say those awful words: *I'm so sorry for your loss.*

At the entrance, all was chaos. One by one, the military divers and SEALs emerged from the darkness, though by all accounts a number of them had been fortunate during their retreat from Tham Luang. As the SEALs arrived at dive base, the pumps holding the water at bay in chambers two and three had broken down. The flood rose quickly and there was barely any time for the rescue personnel to escape before dive base was cut off entirely. Miraculously, everybody was able to make it out, avoiding the drama of our first few days in Thailand when we'd had to manage those four engineers to safety after their ill-advised napping session.

Later, as we celebrated, I wondered how the Wild Boars were getting on. Reports came through to the group that all were being treated in Chiang Rai hospital and had been doing well. They had been admitted to an isolation ward and would have to remain inside for a number of days until the possible contraction of some form of *cave disease* could be ruled out – whatever that meant. If there really was anything contagious living in the waters at Tham Luang, the British divers should have been resting on the same ward as the Wild Boars. We'd been in and out of the filth more than anybody.

Drama soon became a familiar backdrop to my life. In the rush to get home, it was a struggle to keep hold of our diving equipment, as several international diving groups tried to depart at the exact same time. Identifying similar-looking cylinders and fins quickly became an art form. The airport was no cakewalk either: I'd long maintained a habit of keeping back a set of clean clothes during missions, so I could at least arrive home smelling as fresh as possible for my family. (A challenge during any long-haul flight.) All that remained in my rucksack was an old *Shaun the Sheep* t-shirt, a pair of jeans and some clean pants and socks.

Sartorially, I had made a misstep. When the doors at arrivals at Heathrow Airport slid open, I was dazzled by what looked like a wall of exploding camera flashes and screaming and shouting people. Most of them were media; some of them were well-wishers, and when a Thai woman bearing a box of chocolates broke from the crowd to hug me, I knew the events in Tham Luang had taken on a life of their own. The boys had become an international concern, and the world, by the looks of it, had been holding its breath regarding their survival. Even though we'd been questioned by journalists in Tham Luang, this aspect had passed us by. We had been so close to the action it was hard to comprehend the impact of our work.

Surrounded by media, I gave a brief press statement, hoping to avoid the hassle of being questioned on my doorstep over the coming days. (Though it didn't stop a small group from hovering at the drive for hours and days on end anyway. Or a small mountain of *Shaun the Sheep* merchandise from being delivered.) I tolerated a few selfies, comfortable in the fact that unlike my outward-bound journey, I had completed the job as promised. Shortly afterwards, I headed west on the M4. By the afternoon, I was back at the office, adjusting my glasses and looking at spreadsheets; running the IT company and very much restored to a more familiar Clark Kent-style existence – a life that was entirely ordinary.

That concept of normality would come to be stretched to its limits during the next few weeks and months. There were interview requests and demands for personal appearances. Some of them I felt uncomfortable with and declined; others I was happy to do. Within the latter bracket was the previously mentioned meeting with the prime minister, Theresa May, at 10 Downing Street. The other accepted RSVP was the *Pride of Britain Awards, 2018* – an event with plenty of charitable kudos. But given I'm not a great lover of surprises, I became a little uncomfortable when it was announced the Wild Boars were set to be in England around the same time. Apparently they had been invited to watch Manchester United play during the weekend before the awards, and it was hard not to suspect a photo-op reunion was being schemed. The boys didn't owe me anything; I certainly didn't want to be forced front and centre in front of a room full of TV cameras and celebrity figures, or to have the kids trotted out as if they were public property. I told the producers that I was happy to meet the Wild Boars on the night, but if a surprise meeting was coordinated onstage, I would very much walk off it. I was branded a flight risk from then on.

A backstage meeting was eventually fixed before the show

began and that was enough for me. Guessing that the boys, or their parents, would have arranged for some gifts to be brought over, I took the opportunity to have thirteen sweatshirts with the logo of the Cave Diving Group printed across the front. It was just a token gesture to recognise their first 'cave dive', but it felt important to even up the situation in some way. But as we made our way into the Grosvenor Hotel for the awards, our group was ushered past twelve Thai lads who were chatting and joking on the pavement outside. The worst-kept secret of the evening had been well and truly blown, but it was good to see them together again, happy and smiling. The last time I had been with the Wild Boars as a group was in the gloom of chamber nine, when their chances of survival had hung by a thread. The fact that all of them had made it out alive and were now messing around in London seemed miraculous.

Talking and smiling backstage for a few minutes was enough for me. Those kids had their lives to lead and I had mine. They didn't owe us anything and they never had. If anything, the opposite was true: my happiness was drawn from the fact they were still in one piece, and so was I.

IT'S OK TO DO OK

Happiness is a strange thing to define. We all seem to know it when we feel it, but explaining the concept is so much more complex. Countless books have been written on how to achieve happiness; universities around the world have set specific definitions and scales to measure it. Meanwhile, society seems to suggest happiness is a *thing*, a tangible prize, and having achieved it, that *thing* is ours to keep forever. But nothing could be further from the truth. To me, life is about balance: it's important for us to appreciate the good times, but also to accept the dark moments when they arrive, because our existence can often swing between the two in the most unexpected ways. Without valleys, there can never be peaks. Embracing both helps us to move between them.

Of course, it's great to have plans and ideas for the future, goals to aim for and targets to achieve, but I have found that being too rigid as to what those things should look like can lead to disappointment. Planning for a career and imagining yourself in a certain situation is fine. Imagining an upcoming holiday can be a motivator, but if our expectations are too fixed, or inflexible, we might find ourselves destined for disappointment. Reality almost always ends up differing from what we imagined – not better, not worse, *just different*. But if we can take the time to accept and enjoy whatever life gifts us, both the downs as well as the ups, then perhaps a quieter happiness is possible, maybe without all the bells and whistles, but instead with a calmness and a quiet acceptance.

What I have learned is that we are the inventors of our benchmarks and targets, in effect the goals that we hope will make us happy. For example, if our ambition is to swim around a certain chunk of the British coastline and we do so without smashing any records, then that's enough – especially if we enjoyed the process. If we set out to make a homemade movie on YouTube for friends and it ends up getting ten likes rather than ten million, that's also great. Similarly, my aim in the Tham Luang rescue was to bring out as many kids out as was safely possible, without injuring myself or anyone else. I didn't imagine being heralded as a hero afterwards; simply not making a mistake was enough and because I hadn't fantasised about the endgame too much, I remained flexible when the results came in.

In the end, I did OK. And OK was enough.

I have found that a quiet personal satisfaction, although less immediate and much less public than the buzz provided by online likes or kudos on social media, is much more fulfilling than the continual chase of approval from others. The truth is, I accidentally found my role as cave diver because it was fun. I didn't choose or set out to be good at something. Instead I followed my heart towards an activity that interested and excited me. I am a lot less accomplished at climbing, cycling and running, but ultimately each one of those activities has also provided a similar level of satisfaction at different times in my life, and all run along a similar theme: I find joy in movement, but also in the planning and logistics that enable those experiences. I love the process. And any positive results thereafter are a happy consequence.

Of course, I get disappointed when things don't work out quite as I'd have liked. As I have said previously in the book, cave diving is in many ways a game of disappointment and when I've turned around underwater due to safety concerns, there has often been a sinking feeling afterwards or periods of self-doubt. *Should I have gone further?* During those moments, I have worked hard to course correct and say, 'Yeah, I could possibly have achieved more. But I'll accept the decision, because I can go back in next time . . .'

As you might have guessed from some of the statements in this book, I find it very difficult to accept success. Even the idea that I could be considered grown up or responsible, let alone successful, seems very alien to me. But, like happiness, success is a very subjective and transient concept, one that society tries to push onto us from a very young age. Is someone who qualifies as a doctor or a lawyer successful? Does that mean the rest of us aren't? I guess looking back on both my professional life, as well as my hobbies, I could be considered a success. But I prefer to look on it simply as this: *I did OK at the time and mostly I enjoyed it*. That seems like a much more comfortable and realistic view for me to take.

But while I feel it's important not to expect praise for my actions, and it's OK not to *want* praise, I accept that there are times when I have to put myself forward as being the best person for a task or role. When it came to rescuing the boys in Tham Luang, I stepped forward because I genuinely believed that Rick and I were the best placed people to give the boys a chance. That belief, thankfully, turned out to be well founded.

DEFINE YOUR OWN HAPPINESS: THE CHECKLIST

- Be kind to yourself. You are doing OK!
- Choose your own goals. Celebrate your achievements.
- Be present. Live in the moment.

END NOTE
FULL CIRCLE

I accept that I have written *Thirteen Lessons That Saved Thirteen Lives* from a position of privilege, and I don't underestimate my good fortune. For starters, I was exceptionally lucky as a boy. The Scouts gave me a set of experiences that undoubtedly shaped my life and then set me on a path towards the outdoors. Suddenly, I was presented with an environment in which a goofy child who couldn't kick a football was able to find his feet. Previously, I'd only tripped over them. Sometimes I'll revisit the past so I can plot some of the key turning points and many of the earliest ones occurred during my years in Cubs, Scouts and Venture Scouts. I was shown a kindness by the leaders that was above and beyond, and I am absolutely aware of how fortunate I was.

Weirdly, I've never considered myself good with children, nor have I found working with a group of them easy – I have no idea how teachers hold it together. But over the last ten years, I have been trying to repay some of the kindness shown to me. Sharing some of the lessons that so positively impacted upon me seemed like a good way of giving back. I have introduced boys and girls in the Scouts, Beavers, and Cubs to caving. I wanted to share with them the joy I felt when venturing underground for the first time, and it has been satisfying to watch them overcome their fears, learn how to look after one another and work as a team. Maybe their interest in caving will end once they reach adulthood. Maybe, like me, a spark of inspiration will have been lit somewhere. Either way, we'll have all gained. The process for me is rewarding – sometimes stressful, but that's par for the course.

The challenge of cave exploration continues, too: the joy of tinkering with equipment for the next trip is always present, as is the commitment to submerging underground with an interesting objective in mind. The camaraderie and bonds forged through shared experiences remains strong and I carry on learning about both myself, and life. But rescue operations were always only an occasional sideline and it seems to me that any semi-responsible adult or parent would want to offer assistance to others during their time of need. I'm certain that a time will come again when I'm asked to help, as I was in Tham Luang, and I'll be both ready and willing.

Likewise, it's only a matter of time before your next challenge finds *you*. When it does, I hope some of what's been written in these pages will be useful. When the moment comes, remember that it doesn't matter if you believe yourself to be capable. (You really are.) What matters is that you act. Step on the travelator, trust in yourself and be the best you can be. Then swim towards your doubts because that's where the most important self-discoveries are made.

To start, you really only need ask one simple question.

Why not?

THE THIRTEEN LESSONS

#1 START WITH *WHY NOT?*

- Think positive. Reframe the question.
- Remember your talents. Ignore the Inner Critic.
- Take your first step. Board the travelator.

#2 LISTEN TO THE QUIET VOICE

- Listen for warnings. Learn your personal cues.
- Evaluate safety margins. Stay within your limits.
- Know when to stop. Lose a battle to win the war.

#3 ZOOM IN, ZOOM OUT

- Look up and around. Watch the big picture.
- Avoid overfocus. Don't get fixated.
- Understand your capacity. Allocate awareness appropriately.

#4 REST AND DECOMPRESS

- Take time out. Draw fresh inspiration.
- Recognise fatigue. Take time out if necessary.
- Process the past. Translate negative emotions into positive lessons.

#5 ONE BREATH AT A TIME

- Prioritise critical tasks. Start with a breath. (Three seconds.)

- Consider your situation. Make a plan. (Three minutes.)
- Progress towards your goal. Look long term. (Three hours.)

#6 EXPECT THE UNEXPECTED

- Avoid denial. Become comfortably uncomfortable.
- Expect curved balls. Be flexible.
- Go to the *Library Of Plans*. Borrow from the closest option.

#7 STEP UP AND STEP BACK

- Take ownership. Accept responsibility.
- Be realistic. Don't overreach.
- Play to your strengths. Acknowledge your weaknesses.

#8 HARNESSING TEAMWORK AND TRUST

- Select those you trust. Trust those you select.
- Share information. Respect viewpoints.
- Delegate responsibility. Steer only when necessary.

#9 HURRY UP . . . AND DO *NOTHING*

- Allow volatile situations to settle. Don't stir the silt.
- Take action only if it moves you towards your goal. Otherwise, pause.
- Embrace uncertainty. Remember, the zero risk option doesn't exist.

#10 KEEP IT SIMPLE

- Define appropriate reliability. Don't

overcomplicate the plan.

- Understand the cost of failure. Calculate the value of reliability.

- Choose the simplest possible solution. *Better* is the enemy of *Good enough*.

#11 REHEARSE. THEN REPEAT

- Understand your plan. Practise, practise, practise.

- Visualise your feelings. Rehearse your reactions.

- Recall the pain of success. Acknowledge the effort required.

#12 MAKE SUCCESS A HABIT

- Gamify chores. Count winning streaks.

- Complete tasks. Don't skip the small ones.

- Create structure, build routine.

#13 DEFINE YOUR OWN HAPPINESS

- Be kind to yourself. You are doing OK!

- Choose your own goals. Celebrate your achievements.

- Be present. Live in the moment.

ACKNOWLEDGEMENTS

With thanks to Matt Allen, the writer, who guided a grumpy engineer through the literary process. Thanks also to Rory Scarfe my agent, Katie Bond the publisher and everyone at Aurum who has worked tirelessly to make this book a success. Special thanks to my brother Mark for diligently reviewing the text.

I'd also like to express my gratitude to everyone who offered words of wisdom, or helped me to better understand myself throughout my outdoor adventures. You know who you are.

John Volanthen
Bristol, 2021

GLOSSARY

- - - - - - - - - -

A-C

100%
Slang for gas mix containing 100% oxygen.

Air
The gas that makes up Earth's atmosphere. Contains roughly 21 per cent oxygen and 79 per cent nitrogen.

Air bell
A pocket of air found in the roof of an otherwise submerged cave.

Bailout
To switch from a primary breathing source, such as a rebreather, to a secondary source, either another rebreather or open-circuit cylinders.

Bailout cylinder
Cylinder of gas carried primarily for use in emergency.

Bends, the
See Decompression sickness

Body board
A small polystyrene surfboard, more usually found at the beach than in caves.

Bottom walking
A method of propulsion where divers wear lead boots and literally walk along the floor underwater. It is associated with commercial diving or very early diving systems.

Boulder choke
A collection of rocks or boulders of varying sizes that block a cave passage. These occur both above and below the waterline.

Canal
Flooded section of cave passage where there is significant air space. Usually has steep sides.

Cave diver
A person who explores flooded caves using scuba-diving equipment.

Chimney
A narrow, steeply ascending tube. (*See* Rift.)

C-D

Closed circuit
Slang term meaning to breathe from a rebreather.

Commercial diver
A diver who is paid to dive and is regulated by legislation, codes and practices.

CPAP
A Constant Positive Air Pressure (CPAP) dive mask. The mask maintains the pressure of gas surrounding the divers face at just above the pressure found at his or her current depth. Should the mask seal be broken, gas is forced out preventing the ingress of water. The positive pressure also supports breathing.

Cylinder
Steel or aluminium tank, holding compressed gas from which a diver breathes.

Decompression
The process of ascending from depth with frequent breaks, preferably in a slow, controlled manner, to allow a diver to expel inert gas from their body. The length and depth of stops depend on exposure to depth and the gas breathed.

Decompression sickness
A condition affecting divers who ascend from depth too fast. Symptoms include pain, often in the joints, and neurological symptoms such as loss of sensation or paralysis.

Decompression stop
See Decompression.

Demand valve
See Regulator.

Dive reel
Spool containing line that can be deployed underwater. Length can vary from a few meters, to over 1 kilometre (0.6 miles).

Dived up
The term used to describe a cave diver who has recent experience underwater and whose skills are sharp.

Diving cylinder
See Cylinder.

Drysuit
A waterproof neoprene or fabric suit with seals around the wrists and neck under which layers of insulating clothing can be worn.

GLOSSARY

D-O

Dry caver

A person who explores caves without using scuba-diving equipment.

Duck

An obstacle in a cave where a passage mostly full of water must be passed using the minimal airspace available. This is most often done face up while 'kissing the ceiling'.

Eddy

The circulating flow of water causing a small whirlpool out of the main flow.

Elbow

The deepest point in a sump.

Fettle

To tinker with, or otherwise prepare diving gear for use.

Fish bowl mask

Old type of diving mask so called as it has a single large pane of glass on the front that magnifies the wearer's face.

Gas

A term used as a catchall to describe the variety of mixes a diver might breathe, including air, oxygen, helium or combinations of all of these.

Guideline

A line laid in a cave passage to lead divers back to the surface.

Karabiner

A lightweight shackle used by climbers to connect ropes and other items together. Also used by cavers to attach equipment about their person.

Lift bag

A tough, nylon air-filled sack that can be used to raise or move heavy objects underwater.

Narcosis

Raptures of the deep, the martini effect. A temporary intoxication due to breathing an inert gas, typically nitrogen, at depth. Also known as Raptures of the deep, the martini effect.

Off-gassing

The process that occurs in the body during decompression.

Open circuit

Slang term for a standard regulator and cylinder.

P-S

Purge button

The purge button, which is positioned on the second stage of a regulator, causes air to rush from the device. This is normally used to clear water in the mouthpiece so a diver can breathe safely from it again.

Rebreather

A device that recycles the diver's exhaled breath, removing carbon dioxide and adding oxygen. Very much more efficient than open-circuit regulators at depth.

Recompression chamber

A closed steel tube in which a diver can be placed under pressure, used in conjunction with breathing oxygen for treatment of the bends.

Regulator

A device used to allow a diver to breathe gas from a cylinder. Usually there are two stages linked by a hose, the first stage is connected to the cylinder, the second is held in the diver's mouth. Exhaled gas is vented into the water, bubbles are produced.

Resurgence

The point water emerges from the ground and leaves a cave system. Sometimes the head of a river. Often known as a spring.

Rift

A cave passage that is relatively high and narrow. Generally, rifts are straight or nearly so and form along joints or faults in the rock.

Saturation diver

A type of commercial diver involved in very long or deep dives. Often lives for weeks at a time in a pressurised chamber between dives.

Scooter

Battery powered device used to tow divers underwater. Also known as diver propulsion vehicle (DPV).

Sherpa

Caver who carries equipment for another caver, usually a diver. Derived from the term used by climbers in the Himalayas.

Side mount

The practice of mounting diving cylinders or other equipment on a diver's sides rather than their back, reducing their profile and allowing passage through small caves.

GLOSSARY

S-W

Silt

Fine particles of mud that often coat the floor and walls of a cave. Underwater these can be easily stirred up reducing visibility rapidly to zero.

Sked

Plastic flexible stretcher used for cave and military rescues. Can be rolled up lengthways for easy transport.

Skip breathing

A pattern of breathing slowly to conserve gas. Not practised often as it can have serious side effects. Not recommended.

Squeeze

A small opening.

Streamway

A section of cave passage in which a small river or stream of often fast-moving water flows.

Sump

A flooded section of cave passage where the water reaches the roof.

Surface controller

Role of a person who remains above ground during a rescue to facilitate situation management, planning and communications.

Swirl chamber

An area where moving water is spun into a whirlpool current by the surrounding rock, which, in turn, causes sediment and silt to gather in the middle as a dome.

Wet notes

Type of waterproof notebook that can be used underwater or in a cave. Usually has a wood-free pencil attached by string.

Wetsuit

A neoprene suit used to keep a diver warm. It works by trapping a layer of water close to the diver's skin.

Wing

Adjustable buoyancy device worn by a diver on their back. Air can be added or removed to alter lift as required.

JOHN VOLANTHEN

John Volanthen began caving with the Scouts at the age of fourteen and is now a record-holding British cave diver who has been at the forefront of underground rescue and exploration for over twenty years. His many awards include the United Kingdom and Commonwealth George Medal, Royal Humane Society bronze medal and Scientific Exploration Society Pioneer with Purpose.

With a background in medical electronics, John runs his own IT business and has invented underwater mapping devices, communications systems and state-of-the-art micro rebreathers, allowing divers to stay underwater longer than was previously possible.

In 2005 at Wookey Hole in Somerset, John Volanthen and his dive partner Rick Stanton advanced the British cave-diving depth record to 90 metres (295 feet). As part of an international team, he set a world record for the longest cave dive from the surface, reaching over 10 kilometres (33,000 feet) in the Pozo Azul cave system in the Rudrón Valley in Spain.

John lives in Bristol and continues to explore and document underwater caves throughout the world. He is always on standby for the next rescue.

READING GROUP GUIDE

1. Why do you think John Volanthen wanted to combine the story of the Tham Luang cave rescue with thirteen life lessons?

2. Before reading *Thirteen Lessons that Saved Thirteen Lives*, how much did you know about cave diving and what did you learn?

3. Why do you think John became a cave diver, despite all the risks and challenges? What is he drawn to most? Does he convey the joy of cave diving?

4. This is a story about courage. What were the most frightening and challenging moments of the rescue for the authorities, divers and boys trapped underground? What moral questions were they wrestling with? How did they overcome their fear?

5. John details his coping techniques for stressful situations and decision-making including asking 'Why not?', listening to the 'Quiet Voice' and 'Hurry up and do nothing.' Which of these resonates most with you?

6. There are many people involved in the rescue described in this book – who will you remember most and why?

7. Teamwork and trust are essential for cave rescue. How does the book show collaboration working well and breaking down? What barriers to good communication did the Tham Luang rescue face?

8. Is there a scene (or scenes) in *Thirteen Lessons that Saved Thirteen Lives* that will stay with you? What will you remember most vividly?

9. What are your impressions of the author's voice and style? What specific themes does John Volanthen emphasize most throughout the book?

10. How and when does the author use humour to relieve the tension? When does he make you laugh?

11. How does John use visualization to tackle the moral complexities of the rescue?

12. In the End Note, John writes: 'The Scouts gave me a set of experiences that undoubtedly shaped my life.' What childhood experiences have shaped yours?

13. What did you like or dislike most about the book that hasn't been discussed already? Who would you recommend it to and why?

RECOMMENDED FURTHER READING/VIEWING

THE RESCUE (2021, National Geographic Documentary films) – documentary about the Tham Luang cave rescue by Academy Award ® winning *Free Solo* filmmakers Elizabeth Chai Vasarhelyi and Jimmy Chin.

THIRTEEN LIVES (2022, MGM) – major Hollywood motion picture about the Tham Luang cave rescue directed by Academy Award ® winner Ron Howard and starring Colin Farrell as John Volanthen.

THE DARKNESS BECKONS: The History and Development of World Cave Diving by Martyn Farr (2017, Vertebrate Publishing)
John says: 'The definitive book about cave diving, its history and background.'

INDEX

CAVE TUNNELS

- ▬ ▬ FLOODED
- ▬▬ DIVES
- ▬▬ WADING
- ▬▬ DRY SECTIONS

NUMBERS = CHAMBERS/AIR SPACES

∿➤ DIRECTION OF CURRENT

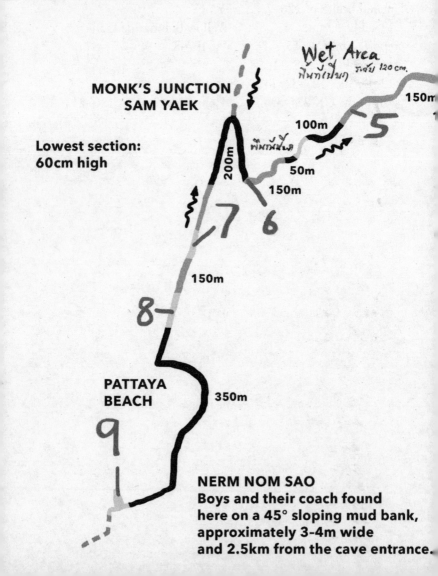

Wet Area
พื้นที่เปียก ระดับ 120 cm.

MONK'S JUNCTION
SAM YAEK

150m

Lowest section:
60cm high

100m

5

200m

พื้นที่เปียก

50m

150m

6

7

150m

8

150m

PATTAYA
BEACH

350m

9

NERM NOM SAO
Boys and their coach found
here on a 45° sloping mud bank,
approximately 3–4m wide
and 2.5km from the cave entrance.